18182

S0-CNH-800

TWAYNE'S WORLD LEADERS SERIES

EDITOR OF THIS VOLUME

Hans L. Trefousse

JOHN ADAMS

TWLS 78

John Adams

JOHN ADAMS

By ROBERT A. EAST

TWAYNE PUBLISHERS

A DIVISION OF G. K. HALL & CO., BOSTON

Published in 1979 by Twayne Publishers,
A Division of G. K. Hall & Co.
All Rights Reserved

Printed on permanent/durable acid-free paper and bound
in the United States of America

First Printing

Library of Congress Cataloging in Publication Data
East, Robert Abraham, 1909-
John Adams.

(Twayne's world leaders series; TWLS 78)
Bibliography: p. 119-23
Includes index.
1. Adams, John, Pres. U. S., 1735-1826.
2. United States—Politics and government—Revolution, 1775-1783.
3. United States—Politics and government—1783-1809.
4. Presidents—United States—Biography.
E322.E27   973.4'4'0924   [B]   79-11181
ISBN 0-8057-7723-7

If rigid moral analysis be not the
purpose of historical writing, there
is no more value in it than in the
fictions of mythological antiquity.
— Charles Francis Adams

Contents

About the Author

Robert Abraham East is a product of the Middle West although he has lived and received degrees in Massachusetts and New York. Born in Lima, Ohio in 1909 he was educated in its public schools and scarcely moved out of town until he went to Williams College at the age of eighteen. His Ph.D. was from Columbia University in 1938. Essentially a teacher of history, he has taught at Columbia University, at the Kansas State College at Emporia, at Brooklyn College and after 1967 at the Graduate Center of the City University of New York. He has also been a Classifier at the National Archives in Washington, D.C., a Rockefeller Fellow at the Council on Foreign Relations, a Fellow of the Newberry Library in Chicago and more recently Executive Director of the Program for Loyalist Studies and Publications, an international organization which has frequently taken him to Canada and England. For many years he conducted an American History contest in Flatbush for the local American Legion. His writing has also been recognized. In 1938 he received the Dunning Prize of the American Historical Association for his *Business Enterprise in the American Revolutionary Era*, and among his many articles are contributions to two *Festschriften* and the life of John Adams in the last edition of the *Encyclopaedia Britannica*. His later books include *John Quincy Adams: The Critical Years, 1785–1794, Connecticut's Loyalists*, and the co-editorship of *The Loyalist Americans, A Focus on Greater New York*. In recent years he has chaired numerous meetings and given addresses about the Loyalists. Most of his time is now spent in Ogunquit, Maine, and his hobby is painting. He and his wife have two children and two grandchildren. He belongs to the American Antiquarian Society, the Colonial Society of Massachusetts, the Maine Historical Society, the Atlantic Association of Historians, the Association for the Study of Connecticut History, the Institute of Early American History and Culture and the Historical Society of Pennsylvania.

Preface

John Adams's favorite subject was himself, but despite his eternal self-examination he apparently had no inferiority feelings at all.

To say that he was self-confident, as well as fascinating and patriotic, does not mean, however, that he ever developed a clear understanding of American politics. He had little grasp of the party system which the American Revolution made inevitable, or of the nature of public opinion upon which it had fed and which it encouraged. He was essentially a builder of governments, although his "checks and balances" seem to have expired today and his old Puritan vision of "a city set upon a hill" quite irrelevant to the modern political process. He was also a much traveled man in spite of his provincialism, and the first to demonstrate the curious fact that many of our much-criticized Presidents have been unusually successful in foreign affairs.

The real John Adams was a bundle of contradictions. Ambivalent in character, he was an ink-loving scribbler in addition to being a learned man, and a non-political politician as well as a good dirt farmer, one who could rejoice in the size of his manure pile and enjoy a tankard of hard cider each morning before breakfast.

The difficulty in writing a biography of John Adams is that which confronts the biographer of anybody, namely the tendency to act like a Recording Angel. This I have tried to avoid. The age of any biographical subject also has to be considered, as well as the age of the author himself, or herself. For example, I doubt whether a young person can ever write about anyone in old age, although the reverse is not true since the elderly can (or should) remember that they were once young. Then, there is always the question as to how thoroughly the history of the period in which the subject lived has been examined. A person should be judged by the standards of his or her own time, although the author may live at a time with quite different standards of which he or she cannot help but be aware.

This biography is based on almost half a century of teaching, reading, and writing about history, especially American history. All this of course has been in the twentieth century. This has been a curious period of time. Some of us have lived through two "World Wars," in addition to all the "little wars," and in spite of our declared intention in 1928, along with so many other nations, to "outlaw" war (The Kellogg-Briand Pact). The isolation of the eighteenth century can be tolerated no longer, and John Adams probably would agree as long as a need for strength is recognized. We will get involved in world affairs anyway, and our only alternative to an effective internationalism is "imperialism." Foreign affairs is our Achilles Heel.

In preparing this biography use has not been made of the microfilmed Adams Papers except for what has been published elsewhere, and for what the author remembers from the preparation of his *John Quincy Adams: The Critical Years, 1785-1794* (Bookman Associates, New York, 1962). It follows the author's sketch of John Adams in the last (fifteenth) edition of the *Encyclopaedia Britannica,* but printed primary and secondary materials have been reexamined. Notes for each chapter and a bibliography are appended.

My indebtedness is great to Professor Hans L. Trefousse, a good friend and colleague for many years. The manuscript was prepared largely because of his interest.

I am also indebted to my son, Frank, for his critical reading of some of these chapters, and to "Tib," my wife of forty-five years, for her customary patience.

ROBERT A. EAST

Ogunquit, Maine

Chronology

1797-1801	Second President of the United States
1800	Makes peace with France
1801-15	First phase of retirement in Quincy
1805	Writes *Autobiography*
1809-12	Sends material to Boston *Patriot*
1816-26	Second phase of retirement in Quincy
1818	Death of Abigail
1820	Attends convention to revise Massachusetts constitution
1826	Dies on Fourth of July on same day as Thomas Jefferson

CHAPTER 1

The Father of the Man

"What would you do Child?"

LITTLE is known about the infancy of John Adams save that he was born in an oldfashioned New England farmhouse with a "leanter," in the North Precinct (now Quincy) of the Town of Braintree, Massachusetts, on October 19, 1735. That was the old style reckoning, however, and when the new style Gregorian calendar was later adopted this made October 30 his true birthday, as he always thereafter recorded.[1] In any case he was born under the sign of Scorpio, i.e., one destined to strife, as perhaps the neighbors noted.[2]

One assumes that little John Adams must have been one of the lustiest babies ever known; and what is even more certain is that his fairy godmother, or some other well-disposed person, must have tossed into his cradle exactly the right combination of genes and chromosomes to make for future greatness.

The parents of this bright boy, the first of their three sons, were forty-four-year-old Deacon John Adams of Braintree, a small-scale farmer and cordwainer (a maker of shoes and other leather products), and selectman of the Town of several generations of thrifty yeomen there; and Susanna Boylston of Brookline, a brisk young woman of twenty-five of a family with a touch of distinction such as John Adams always seemed to crave. Indeed, the Boylston coat of arms was to be used briefly by his family half a century later.

Father Adams seems to have been rather a quiet but steadfast person of charitable disposition, "The Honestest Man I ever knew," his eldest son once said.[3] The more emotional mother was not without her charms (she was in time to marry a second husband), although she apparently had a blundering way of asking questions.[4] Both must have made excellent parents. All three of their sons were to

15

grow to manhood as was not always the case in those days of frequent births and deaths.

From his parents John inherited a rather short and stocky person (he was five feet seven or nine inches tall in manhood, he once guessed), and no doubt many other sturdy qualities. Yet in early childhood the mother must have been the principal focus of attention. Adams was later to recall the visits he had made as a child to her old home in Brookline.[5]

To the younger brothers who eventually came along—Peter Boylston, born two years later, who was to live to a ripe if deaf and blind old age, and little Elihu in 1741, who was to die of dysentery in 1775—the older brother, Johnny or Jack, must have been a great boy, indeed, one to be obeyed, admired, and perhaps even a little feared. The family farmhouse must have been a most active place for the growing family, with the bustling mother ever present and perhaps a servant girl. No doubt it was often a chilly, or even freezing, place, with open fires always to be attended.

Deacon Adams may have been a small farmer but he had accumulated considerable property. Peter was eventually to inherit the old homestead and its thirty-five acres, but not the smaller house next to it which eventually went to John and where his early married life was spent. Elihu was to get his third of the personal property and still another farm. John was to buy the old homestead back from Peter some years later.[6]

The reasons for this division of property was that John, as the oldest, seems to have been destined from birth to get a higher education, as had his uncle Joseph, an older brother of Deacon Adams, who had graduated from Harvard and had once taught in the local school. He had subsequently become a clergyman in nearby New Hampshire.

Perhaps the family's emphasis on education is best given in John Adams's *Autobiography:*

As my Parents were both fond of reading, and my father had destined his first born, long before his birth to a public Education I was very early taught to read at home and at a School of Mrs. Belcher the Mother of Deacon Moses Belcher, who lived in the next house on the opposite side of the Road.

At the age of seven the boy also read a list of advice for children which his Grandmother Bass had drawn up in her own handwriting and which he thought "wonderfully fine." It may also be mentioned that it was to this Grandmother Bass (his father's mother) that John Adams later attributed some of his life-long love of reading. He was told that the old lady possessed more love of literature than was common to most women of her station in that day, and that she had always been a "diligent reader" as well as a most exemplary person.[7]

In religious matters it should never be forgotten that Father Adams was a Deacon in the local church and presided over family prayers, in addition to reading aloud each Sunday from Willard's *Body of Divinity.*

The most important kind of religious instruction that little John Adams must have experienced was in the local meetinghouse, then presided over in congregational matters in the North Precinct by the Reverend Mr. Hancock. Since Hancock's pastorate did not end until his death in 1744, when John was nine years old, one can assume that the boy's earliest religious instruction must have been more-or-less Calvinistic. Adams once referred to himself as a "church-going animal" from birth, and recalled how he had once gazed in awe at the venerable heads in the front benches of the meetinghouse.[8]

The young man, a Mr. Briant, who succeeded the Reverend Mr. Hancock, proved to be something of an "Arminian" in religion (he was also a friend of the noted Jonathan Mayhew in Boston), which meant that he paid little attention to "irresistible grace," and more to "good works" than to traditional Predestinarianism.[9] Unfortunately, the "good works" apparently did not extend to his wife who subsequently "eloped" from his bed and board, and this, together with theological matters, raised quite a storm in Braintree a few years later, even disturbing young Adams at Harvard. Even as an older boy, however, he must have been considerably influenced by the ideas of Mr. Briant, in those days of reaction to the Great Awakening which had recently swept all New England with its revival of Calvinism and "enthusiasm" (i.e., evangelism).

All this must have accounted in one way or another for those "Moral Sentiments and Sacred Principles" which John Adams tells us he had endeavored to preserve all his life, along with the conditions of "the times and the Country in which I was born and the Curcumstances which surrounded me. . . ."[10]

Here, however, is also a partial explanation of that ambivalence of character that was later to distinguish John Adams: the uneasy combination of his earliest religious instruction with the more "advanced" ideas he was later to encounter.[11] But everything originally must have been quite simple and admonitory in the Adams family.

The congregational structure, in winter as chilly as a barn, was also the place for local political meetings and was commonly known as the "meeting-house." Town meetings were held about three times a year, with special meetings inbetween. Adams once said that the typical New Englander was a product of such affairs. All social distinctions were considered inconsistent with the spirit of the town. Officers were elected at these affairs (a treasurer, constables, hog-callers, field-viewers, etc.), sometimes enabling the town to collect fines when persons refused office; and all local taxes were levied there.[12] Since benches were often overturned in the heat of these political meetings, the interior of the meetinghouse must often have become respectable only on Sundays.

Politics and religion were still closely related and church discipline still a powerful factor in town affairs, taking oversight of many private problems, such as drunkenness, domestic discord, and, above all, incontinence. Self-criticism was emphasized, for what was considered criminal in one was considered criminal in all. Heaven may have been close at hand, but so was Hell. Such religious supervision may seem today to have bordered on tyranny, but we may be sure that little John Adams, along with many grownups, never questioned its wisdom.[13]

Much of what John Adams was later to learn about the world must have been based on what he learned as an unsophisticated boy in that little world of Braintree, on the South Shore of Massachusetts only ten miles away from Boston.

Braintree was basically a farming community, although it had some fishing, and the land was tolerable if one makes allowance for the outcropping of granite. It was also plentifully supplied with "tippling" houses, unusual in number even for those hard-drinking days, and despite its sturdy individualism to have cherished ideas of social distinction as demonstrated by the importance of several branches of the "genteel" Quincy family. There was a considerable number of "Churchmen" in Braintree who attended the Episcopal Church and who duly said prayers for the King. Indeed, the North Precinct had the reputation of being somewhat "Toryish," and it had been selected as a target for "missionary" work by the English (Anglican) Society for Propagating the Gospel, no doubt to the amusement as well as to the consternation of many.[14]

Some children like little John Adams long remembered the frightening days of a threatened "invasion" during the "Old French War" (i.e., "King George's War"),[15] although all must have known about the local militia. They must also have heard those "wise saws and ancient maxims" which Braintree, like all country communities, no doubt treasured; and they must have heard of a vague tradition concerning the riotous Thomas Morton and his infamous maypole which the Puritans had long ago cut down. Indeed, not far from the site of that ancient scandal of Merrymount and its band of "gallant vagabonds" stood Mount Wollaston itself, the home of old Colonel John Quincy, the leading political and social figure of the town (whose name was later given to the North Precinct) and presently the grandfather of little Abigail Smith of nearby Weymouth.

Meanwhile, young John Adams was growing up into one of the most vigorous of boyhoods. He wandered through fields and marshes, enjoying shooting and all kinds of sports. Let him again be quoted:

> ... I spent my time as idle Children do in making and sailing boats and Ships upon the Ponds and Brooks, in making and flying Kites, in driving hoops, playing marbles, playing Quoits, Wrestling, Swimming, Skaiting and above all in shooting, to which Diversion I was addicted to a degree of Ardor which I know not that I ever felt for any other Business, Study or Amusement.

All this he attributed to the indolence of his teacher in the local Latin school, a Mr. Joseph Cleverly, a tolerable scholar and gentleman but a most indolent man in the opinion of young Adams, who must have attended the public school for several years after learning his ABC's from Dame Belcher. Cleverly seems to have scolded him severely only once, when he found out that the boy brought his gun to school; but in this the teacher may have been ahead of the times and was merely giving the boy his head in allowing him to do as he pleased as an occasional truant.[16] Indeed, it is interesting that Cleverly should have been keeping the public school at all, since he was one (though not the first) of those dreaded Churchmen ("Episcopalians") said to be the foe of all Congregationalists ("Presbyterians"), of that High Church or Anglican breed which constituted about an eleventh of the three hundred and fifty families in the North Precinct, and which, as already noted, had selected Braintree as a place appropriate for "missionary" activities.

Young Adams's enthusiasm for sports, and above all for shooting, must often have been given expression after school or in summertime. He even saw some of the local Indians in their wigwams, and "chiefs" sometimes visited his father's house.[17] He enjoyed scenes of violence, in addition to shooting birds and squirrels, and tells us that he had loved to see boys fighting as well as cock-fighting; and that he had once seen two rams butting each other until one broke the other's skull, and (though it had been a "dredful, cruel fight") had enjoyed it.[18]

It probably was in many ways a typical farm boyhood. One recalls what a New England poet later said of another Barefoot Boy:

> When all the things I heard or saw,
> Me, their master, waited for.

Unfortunately, John Adams never was to become a poet, and one can only hope that his love of nature was always broad and true; but it must be admitted that he loved his gun as a boy, and that he even became acquainted with tobacco (whether chewing or smoking is not clear) when once skating on a neighborhood pond. The tobacco habit, by the way, he was to retain in one form or another throughout most of his life.[19]

Whether this vigorous boy ever went barefoot in summertime we do not know, although it should not be forgotten that his father made shoes in winter. We also do not know whether the boy ever initiated his younger brothers into outdoor sports, or into the manly art of using tobacco. Young Elihu, at least, must have been too young for the latter.

This robust youth was to settle into serious study at about the age of puberty, but it is worth noticing that from ten or eleven years of age he had been very fond of the company of girls. This was not a particularly unusual thing, especially since Deacon Adams's boys had no sister, and probably meant no more than showing off bareback horseriding to the accompaniment of female admirers' cheers; but the fact that he was to mention it in his *Autobiography* shows that it must have meant a great deal to him. He was proudly to recall that despite this "amorous disposition," his affection for his youthful flames had never been accompanied by any incontinence, which he says he controlled throughout his college years and for several years after; but he complained that female attraction had engaged him too much until he was married in 1764.

Indeed, he was to state bluntly in old age that no matron or virgin had ever had cause to blush at his sight, or to regret his acquaintance.[20]

The early fondness for girls and a love for the out-of-doors, and perhaps for the ever-present farm "chores," was attended by a certain neglect of books. The boy seemed to detest one Latin grammar in particular. The Father was alarmed and frequently remonstrated with the boy, who replied to the question, "What would you do Child?" by answering, "Be a Farmer."[21]

The Father attempted to show him how hard a life that was by taking him to get some thatch from a nearby muddy place; but the boy survived the work and consented to return to his books only on condition that he be sent to another school. If he were revolting against his father, this was a very natural thing. To his wish the Father eventually consented, and John was accordingly sent to a private school kept by a certain Mr. Marsh, the son of a former minister, who had a good name for getting scholars into Harvard where he had several relatives. The boy now began to study in earnest, relaxing his zeal for his fowling piece. He was obviously taking a "cramming" course, but also making a first step in dissipating an inclination for sports and female distractions, as he was later to describe study at college.[22] Books were apparently a good substitute for girls.

This conversion of John Adams into a serious scholar must have taken place at around the age of fourteen. He was to spend only about a year and a half with Marsh, who cared little for farm life or for religion, but much for the history of England and of course for the preparation of his students. The boy was to enter college while still amazingly young (although not as young as some). College in those days must have been something like a "prep" school today, although it should be remembered that "young" men in the eighteenth century appeared much "older" than they do today and dressed accordingly.

When being interviewed at Harvard, this vigorous and well educated boy had to meet the President and tutors alone, since Marsh did not show up to introduce him as he had promised. It was the first of several embarrassing experiences of a similar nature which Adams eventually was to encounter. He never was one to lack self-confidence if given half a chance, however, and while being interviewed and asked to make a rather difficult translation from Latin, he was greatly relieved when permitted to use a dictionary.[23] The result must have been quite satisfactory, for the boy returned home, rejoicing.

CHAPTER 2

Education

"I soon perceived a growing Curiosity"

THE entrance of that country boy John Adams into the
"University at Cambridge" in 1751 plunged him into a life of
sophisticated learning such as he had never known, save possibly for
his "cramming" experience during the preceding year or so in
Braintree.

Harvard, as it was commonly called, was still primarily a place
for training schoolmasters and clergymen despite its sprinkling of
scions of officialdom and of mercantile families. It was still as
independent in spirit and ardent in learning as the Puritans had
intended it to be when they had founded the place. Puritans had
always encouraged outspokenness, although this freedom became
unforgivable if it proved to be heretical. They had believed in
learning, and not in some "inner light."

Cambridge in the late eighteenth century was not only about the
same size as Braintree but also just as rural. Even the college
professors kept cows.[1] Cambridge also reflected some of those
distinctions which Braintree knew, as seen in the "rank" into which all
college freshmen were classified each spring. Young Adams was
placed fourteenth in a class of twenty-eight, an idea which must have
appeared quite natural to him, even if the rank was not entirely
satisfactory to his mother.[2]

On entering the "seminary" our young country scholar was
confronted with a life so routine as to have bordered on the monastic.
He lived in Massachusetts Hall for all four years, while classes, the
library, and scientific apparatus were in nearby Harvard Hall.
Following daily prayers at six o'clock there was a bread and milk
breakfast, frequently supplemented by richer fare for wealthier

students. At noon dinner there were meat and vegetables, and there was provided some kind of a supper at night. Classes were held from eight o'clock until noon, followed by about two hours of out-of-door activities. Evening prayers were said at five o'clock. Study was primarily in the evenings when candles were the only available illumination. Privies were out-of-doors, of course, and all heat came from using firewood, which for Adams was carted from Braintree by his brother Peter. There never seemed to be enough wood.

The curriculum was still basically classical, but the President gave theological instruction each Saturday morning. Themes and theses were requirements for all classes, and young John Adams throve on the system. He soon "perceived a growing Curiosity, a Love of Books, and a fondness for Study," which completely "dissipated" his old inclination for sports and for female society.[3]

The freshman year for all students consisted of study under the guidance of a resident tutor (Joseph Mayhew in the first term and "Father" Flynt in the second), in logic, rhetoric, Latin, and Greek, each taught by one of the four tutors of the college. Not until his sophomore year did young Adams get a taste of advanced logic under the celebrated Professor Wigglesworth, and not until he was a junior did he have "Natural Philosophy," i.e., mathematics, climatology, and physics, under the equally celebrated Professor Winthrop.

Adams was to recall years later that mathematics and natural philosophy had been his particular interest at Harvard, a choice that he later regretted since they subsequently had been of so little use to him, but he seems never to have considered becoming a regular student of the subject.[4]

The "Enlightenment" of the time, of which Adams must have got a taste at Harvard, combined with his love of science must have led him to look for "laws" everywhere, as "Social Darwinism" was to do for many a century later.

Winter vacation at Harvard began in January and lasted for six weeks, while summer recess was approximately for the same length of time, classes resuming in September. When the college was closed in the spring of 1752 because of a smallpox epidemic, a change occurred. Together with the loss of eleven days because of the adoption of the Gregorian calendar, this resulted in the winter vacation being eliminated altogether the following year.[5]

During vacation periods young Adams must commonly have gone back to his father's farm in Braintree, although we know that during the summer of 1753, together with a cousin he visited as far north as his Reverend Uncle Joseph's in Newington, New Hampshire, next door to Portsmouth.[6]

The college itself was presided over by wise President Edward Holyoke ("Old Guts"), a distinguished Latinist as well as theologian,[7] who was responsible for the general conduct of his ninety-odd charges, with particular attention to the enforcement of a strict code of fines for all kinds of misbehavior. "Profane swearing," for example, was listed at five shillings, and there were even more "atrocious" crimes. All students were obviously expected to conduct themselves properly.

This raised difficulties for some of the more high spirited students, who frequently had plenty of money to spend. Drinking, card playing, and visiting nearby Boston were not unknown. Not all students were like John Adams in having had a frugal farm background. Some had very fancy notions as to dress as well as deportment.

It is interesting to notice the kind of company young Adams kept. The flashier type of student he apparently eschewed, for his closest friends were more or less like himself, i.e., destined for the ministry or for some other kind of learning, and no doubt all accustomed to a sober way of life. Such friends in his own class included Moses Hemmingway, who was one day to become a distinguished preacher, and Sam Locke, a future if only brief-in-office President of Harvard. Other close friends included Sam West, a future chaplain in the Continental army, and David Treadway, subsequently a professor of Mathematics at King's College in New York, both of whom were in the class ahead. He also knew his cousin Webbs. However, John was on especially good terms with the fashionable and kindly Sam Quincy of Braintree, with well-born John Wentworth of Portsmouth, with high-ranking William Browne, and with that sickly young patrician, Philip Livingston of Albany.[8]

Sam Quincy in particular seems to have been John Adams's good friend at Harvard (and of course the brother of that tomboy, Hannah Quincy, whom Adams already knew in Braintree and whom he was to come so perilously close to marrying years later). It is curious that Sam Quincy, like Wentworth and Browne, should eventually have turned out to be Loyalist in politics, and later to have differed so markedly from John Adams in his Revolutionary enthusiasm. Even the lowly Jacob Bailey, last in "rank" in the class of 1755, while also aiming at the ministry was eventually to do so as a missionary in the Anglican church, and to become still another Loyalist.

Of course there were other Harvard men known to young Adams, many of whom like some of his closest friends were to remain more or less sympathetic with his later political principles. There was the foppish John Hancock who had also originated from Braintree and whom Adams knew from childhood[9] but had been adopted by a rich uncle in Boston; also a future U.S. Senator, Tristram Dalton of Newburyport; and the future distinguished lawyer, David Sewall of York, Maine. Young Adams seems to have made friends with all kinds of students at college from all levels of society, and with young men later representative of all shades of political opinion.

What kind of ideas did young John Adams hold in college, and what kind of a person was he becoming?

Since his college themes have long since been destroyed, one of our few insights lies in the affairs of a declaiming society—a "play-reading Club"—he was invited to join as a junior and senior sophister. There he eventually seems to have become acknowledged as a real dramatic speaker, obviously loving all forms of dramatic declamation and striving to execute them vigorously.[10] He had also learned to detest bigotry and perhaps to have become sympathetic with "Arminian" leanings in theology, or at least sympathetic with the right of people to think about religion. Perhaps he was already on the road which was finally to take him into cherishing little more of Christian thought than is to be found in the Sermon on the Mount.

This "liberal" attitude was revealed in his sympathy with the Reverend Mr. Lemuel Briant, the preacher in the First Church in Braintree, when that person's personal and theological difficulties culminated in 1753.[11] Certainly young Adams did not agree with his Uncle Eb's tendency to lump all theological questions together with Briant's problems of personal conduct. Uncle Eb, who had once made a loan to help pay for John's entrance to Harvard, was eventually faced with the choice of either confessing in open-church meeting his error of gossiping scandal or of being denied access to the Communion Table. Apparently he chose the latter, at least at first. While most young people in Braintree sympathized with young Mr. Briant rather than with Uncle Eb, so also did old Colonel John Quincy along with other Quincys. Many of the "gentry" seem to have demonstrated a capacity to be broadminded in matters of faith and morals.

Yet a certain scorn for evangelical religious practice is also shown in Adams's "noisy imitation" at Harvard of the Reverend White-field's preaching,[12] which had continued the so-called "Great Awakening." There is no evidence, however, that young Adams ever attended Episcopal (i.e., Anglican) services on Sunday in Cambridge (as was permitted at Harvard to the scandal of many good people) or that he ever took high-church notions seriously. Presumably he was still a good Congregationalist, albeit a somewhat troubled one.

Such doubts may have made him wonder whether he should become a minister at all, although as a senior he was put on the Hollis Scholarship to encourage future ministers, or to turn his thoughts elsewhere, as to medicine or the law.[13] His curiosity and out-spokenness, very natural in an independent young man, no doubt contributed to his ultimate decision about a career.

One circumstance probably reveals an innate political conserva-tism. On graduating from Harvard in 1755, he replied, as a Respondent in Latin, that liberty cannot exist without law. That the two are necessarily connected was to become his life-long conviction.

John Adams is said to have read widely as an undergraduate, and no doubt this is true since he always loved books; but his wider education really began when he started to teach grammar school and to undergo an apprenticeship at law in Worcester, about thirty miles west of Boston. His life at college appeared in retrospect to have been "gorgeous" in its prospects[14] but now he began to see life in broader and harsher terms. Of course, at the age of twenty he was a somewhat older "young" man.

On arriving in Worcester in late 1755, at the invitation of the local minister, to take up his grammar school teaching (which he was to continue in order to support himself when he began to study law), young Adams boarded around as was the custom, even at one time with the family of the local surgeon. He became exposed to the most extreme ideas about religion and even to "Deism" and to books on the subject, and to the company of several of the Town's most "advanced" thinkers. He even heard about the town "crank" who considered any restriction on the suffrage as evidence of the spirit of "anti-Christ." All these most radical notions, of course, were ideas which Adams was later to identify in his *Autobiography* with the ideas of the "wild men of the French Revolution."[15]

All notions of egality raised questions about the gentry con-trol of the Worcester area on the part of the local Chandler family, which had been hospitable to young Adams. He was somewhat embarrassed by this, as he later said was shown in his refusal to practice law in Worcester and to enter local politics there.[16]

Because the Adams diary is available from this point on, it may exert an undue influence on our opinions by placing too much evidence on what the young man encountered after reaching the age of twenty. The diary was the beginning of his life-long love of scribbling, and revealed his innermost thoughts, although his actions may have been a very different thing. The diary also contains enormous gaps, sometimes for as long as two years as when he was studying law,[17] and often tells us only enough to make us long for more. Indeed, it is not really a diary at all but a sort of journal of reflections, and only one man's opinion about anything and everybody. Yet the journal, or diary, does reflect his enormous energy in putting his thoughts on paper.

The diary had actually begun in late 1755, appropriately with an earthquake, as has been remarked, although Adams had already made fumbling starts while still at Harvard. As an upper classman he had begun by making observations about the weather, perhaps as a byproduct of his interest in science. Apparently when he moved to Worcester he was still under the influence of science (as well as critical of Calvinism). Some of the earliest diary entries deal not only with the weather but with the nature of the universe.[18] There is even a notice of someone's false report of the early return of Halley's Comet, although when that spectacular event did finally occur in 1759 Adams seems to have taken little notice of it, except to record such earlier errors.[19] By then he may have been too much taken up with his first efforts at practicing law, although the material in his diary for that period is so scanty as to make this conjectural. In any case, despite his confidence in "reason" he seems later to have lost much of his earlier concern with "natural philosophy," even if it was never forgotten completely. He was always looking for "laws" in something or other, likening them to a clock's.

Such a hangover from his college days is less true of his concern with philosophical interests in general and with religion in particular. His interest in delineating the "character" of the men and women he met is also a very spotty thing. Adams was still in philosophic and religious mood in those early days in Worcester. It was only later that he was to become deeply interested in the "science" of government.

His decision in 1756 to study law with James Putnam, and to live in the Putnam household, must have been an enormous relief. Law he identified with human reason. It was a decision he regretted not having made at college. Even so it raised questions with his family and friends, all of whom still supposed that he would enter the ministry.

Young Adams's concern with "truth" must have had something to do with this decision. Although he was always to regard the law as subject to the same ethical goals as the ministry—to procure a "Redress of Wrongs"—as his correspondence with Jonathan Sewall was later to reveal, this must have meant in some degree the substitution of evidence for "revealed" truth, and of law for "simple" justice. It again illustrates Adams's curiously ambivalent nature, i.e., his ability to keep a foot in several camps, in this case both secular and religious.

When the idea of the ministry, like that of medicine, had once and for all been put aside—"necessity" drove him to it, he said[20]—the young man must have become absorbed in James Putnam's conversation about what constitutes legal "evidence" and with weighty books about the law. Unfortunately, as already noted, the diary tells us nothing about what actually went on in the mind of this young apprentice, although there are several informative letters available. Even what we know about "Old Put" himself (he was actually only about ten years older than Adams) is largely confined to his having been a Harvard graduate and a most sophisticated man as well as a learned lawyer—perhaps the "most learned lawyer in America"— that his wife was a daughter of the Chandler family, and that he eventually became a Loyalist in the American Revolution.

James Putnam presumably enjoyed the company of his bright young boarder and apprentice even though they differed in religion and politics sometimes,[21] but he did not have him sworn in at the local bar when the two years of apprenticeship were over. He even neglected to give Adams a general letter of recommendation (although he seems to have given several Boston Bar members an account of his morals and studies), when the latter decided in 1758 to return to his parents' house in Braintree and to practice law from there. This omission became something of an embarrassment to Adams when he applied for admission in Boston to the Court of Common Pleas in Suffolk County. His treatment rankled at the time, although he was later to give a kindlier account of one of the lawyers who very properly had been critical of his credentials.[22]

John Adams was often to refer to his "friends" in Worcester; the memory of these must have been strong upon him as he returned to Braintree in 1758. Actually he had been home on earlier occasions while teaching and studying in Worcester, for the two towns are only about forty miles apart. Among such friends, perhaps, were those "advanced thinkers" Baldwin and Doolittle; surely the Congregational minister; and certainly Dr. Nahum Willard and his lady; the Putnams; the Chandlers; and probably one Betsy Greene of Bristol, Rhode Island, a sister of Mrs. Chandler and a frequent visitor in Worcester.[23] Adams probably had seen Betsy when he had once stayed over with the Greenes when taking dispatches to Rhode Island's governor, during the recent "French and Indian War."

Although young Adams never engaged in any kind of warfare he had seen a good deal of military display in Worcester during the war with the French, and had rejoiced in Britain's ultimate victory just as he had despaired because of her earlier losses. He had favored the idea of American colonial union in order to make a better Empire, and like James Putnam had favored the putting aside of all colonial disputes for the purpose of winning the war.[24] Unlike Putnam he had not been active in the militia, of which Putnam was at one time commander. He was now also a Master of Arts, having read an address at Harvard at the preceeding commencement (it being just such a simple matter as that, in those days).

One other factor pertinent to these years which should presently be mentioned is Adams's concern with his health while at Worcester, which once resulted in his undertaking a milk diet to which he was to return intermittently during the rest of his life.[25] But this sort of thing, like complaints about one's teeth, must have been quite commonplace for most mortals in the eighteenth century (or in any other century for that matter). Natural, too, was his determination to return to Braintree where he said he enjoyed the salty air and "mountain" breezes, and where his parents had invited him to return. They were obviously glad to have him back and he was glad to rejoin them.

CHAPTER 3

The Critical Years

"A Pen is certainly an excellent Instrument"

WHEN John Adams returned to his parents' house in Braintree in 1759, to practice law occasionally and to read about it voraciously[1] he must have been in a mixed state of mind about many things. Loving to write, he would write on any subject.[2] The diary entries in particular, so informative and amusing, show something bad as well as good in everybody. Even in a land devoted to diary-keeping Adams was in a class by himself. He demonstrated those signs of writing energy that were later to become so remarkable.

These are truly his "critical" years. The young yeoman-lawyer was attracted by the genteel Hannah Quincy, the grownup and elegant sister of Sam,[3] and spent much time at the house of her father, Colonel Josiah Quincy. He started attacking the local tippling houses and all "pettyfogging" lawyers,[4] tried incessantly to write for the newspapers, and finally became reimmersed in the joys of farming, even before his father's death in 1761.[5]

John Adams's experiences in Braintree were to culminate in his marriage in 1764 to Abigail (Quincy) Smith of neighboring Weymouth, surely one of the most glorious marriages ever made. First, however, this restless, scribbling, and self-analytical young man had to be disappointed in love with her cousin Hannah, who had already rejected an older friend of Adams, the English-born Richard Cranch. The latter had then directed his interest elsewhere and had married Mary Smith, an elder sister of Abigail.

Hannah ("Orlinda") Quincy has been called a tireless flirt.[6] It was not until her marriage in 1760, which young Adams regarded rather sourly, remarking upon her husband's brutal character and "rudeness" to her in public, that her many admirers were finally "released."

Perhaps the goodnatured and intelligent Hannah should be given the order of merit for permitting the admiration of both Cranch and Adams to be turned in the direction of her cousin Smiths.[8]

These are also the years when Jonathan Sewall, the future Loyalist but at that time John Adams's best friend at the bar, about whom he already had secret doubts,[9] was coming to Braintree to court Esther Quincy. She was still another cousin of Abigail Smith. Sewall was to marry Esther in 1764, although her sister many years later was to marry the "Whig" John Hancock of Boston, who had been born in Braintree. The Quincy family must have been badly divided in many ways.

The Town of Braintree promptly employed young Adams in many capacities, as in laying out roads and in dividing the common lands. He was always to be a good citizen of the Town and to take his local responsibilities seriously, living up to his father's reputation.

Meantime Adams gloried in the name of Briton,[10] enjoyed the social life in Braintree, and continued his "practicing" law. He also tried continuously to write for the Boston press, as already noted, demonstrating his ambition in that regard.[11] Newspapers, it should be noted, had by now become well-established in many colonial places, although they had been a comparatively recent development in American history. John Adams seems to have found them a constant source of inspiration and temptation, not only because of his love for writing and of making observations about people, but because of a desire to show off the learning which was ever increasing.

His continuing concern with himself and with whatever it is that leads men to fame and greatness, whether it be vanity and fortune or virtue and disinterestedness—questions as to what human nature was, were common themes in the eighteenth century—continued to trouble him. Even "genius" merely seemed to suggest an ability to perceive an order in events.[12] Sooner or later he must have decided that in order to do good, one must also be successful.

His ideas must still have been something of a mixture. He even voted with the newly-formed Boston Bar in 1763 to censure James Otis, Jr. for politicking with "pettifoggers."[13] Young lawyer Adams was later to defend poor Otis when the latter was injured in a tavern brawl with a customs commissioner, and to consider him a great man in spite of his "inconsistencies"; but Adams must have had grave doubts in 1763.

Although within two months of starting to practice law John Adams had drawn a "writ" and within two years had been admitted to the Superior Court, it was not until later that he really entered upon the active phase of his legal career. His marriage in 1764 was unquestionably to have something to do with this eventual success.[14]

Adams's early law "practice" had been notable for his interest in books. His intellectual side was never so well shown as in those years of few cases and ample time for reading. As early as 1761 he purchased books on the law and its history. Almost from the beginning, Coke, Justinian, Vinnius, Bracton, and of course Bolingbroke's *Idea of a Patriot King,* with its denunciation of factional politics, had been among his reading. Coke, in particular, became his master and inspiration. Some of these books he borrowed from the Harvard library and some from fellow lawyers, and their significance is clear: the philosophical importance of the law for politics was from the beginning stressed in Adams's mind. He must have had plenty of time for this despite the active social life that he continued to live in Braintree.

Young Adams also found time for making self-revealing observations in his diary. He frequently reproaches himself for late rising, especially in the early years; but one day he "Rose with the sun. Brot up the Horse and took a Ride over Penns Hill. . . ." On another occasion he reflects, "I feel vexed, fretted, chaffed. . . ," and later, "'Tis impossible to judge with much Precision of the true Motives and Qualities of human actions." He confesses that he had been "stupid to the last Degree, in neglecting to spred my Acquaintance." He reproaches himself, "Why have I not Genius to start some new Thought. Some thing that will surprise the World," and "I feel my own Ignorance, I feel concern for Knowledge, and fame. I have a dread of Contempt, a quick sense of Neglect, a strong Desire of Distinction."[15] His ambition was clearly revealed.

On a later occasion as he lay "abed," he congratulates himself for having been diligent; but on another, "This day has been spent to little Purpose." One night he records, "Have been out of Humour, this Evening, more than I have been some Weeks if not Months. Reflection, thinking on a Girl, ill Health, Want of Business &c., wrought me by insensible degrees in a peevish Mood." Once he finds that he has executed "none" of his plans of study.[16]

Things begin to improve in some ways. He finds in his love of writing that "A Pen is certainly an excellent Instrument, to fix a Mans Attention and to inflame his Ambition." Regarding a scheme to get his brother Peter appointed deputy sheriff, he notes in 1761 that his fears of failing "are at last finished," although "the Passions of the

World" must always be guarded against. In 1762 he significantly records, "My thoughts have taken a sudden turn to Husbandry."[17] This was when he was becoming deeply interested in farming and before he became a really important lawyer. He was then as always a real dirt farmer. One of his later diary entries laconically records "kill'd cow."

In some of his observations Adams discloses interesting political ideas, such as his thoughts on Governor Bernard's address in 1761 and the reply of the General Court. He especially laments that victory at arms is often ignored by treaties, and that "leading" does not necessarily mean "national" advantage (he meant British advantage). In thus noting the importance of treaties he already was showing a concern he was to hold for the rest of his life, and to the eventual benefit of his country.[18]

Much of his incessant but anonymous writing was intended for the newspaper press—apparently fruitlessly until 1763—usually on the subject of tippling houses, i.e., taverns and dram shops, and their close connection with vice, debt, and "claps." Several efforts start out with statements that he himself is an "old Man" turn seventy; and he once refers to himself as a most "tittering, giggling Mortal." Although he once boasted "no tyrant can Lord it over us," he considers human nature basically to be at fault where man's failings are concerned. People of temperance, honor, and sobriety, tend to neglect the shocking things that go on in taverns, he claims.[19]

Apparently he would write about anything. One of his would-be newspaper contributions is to his "Dear Nieces," and affects to contain good advice for their proper behavior![20]

Something like a social "leveling" view is occasionally expressed by this ambitious young man of yeoman extraction. His later concern with "aristocracy" is amusing in this connection. As early as his Worcester days he had resolved "never again" to say envious things about possessors of office, or to try to be witty at the expense of people with "laced Wastecoats or Large Estates." In 1761, on the subject of taxes, in a projected newspaper article he had openly sneered at the activities of "Our Gentry." These are rare examples, however. Even when he argues that a person "of obscure Birth" can only defend himself through the newspaper press, the observation loses most of its significance when it is remembered that he was attempting at the time to have the newspaper accept his contribution.[21] In short, he was indulging in flattery.

What is much more revealing as to the character of this young man is the diary entry where he approves of at least one of Benjamin Prat's ideas: that older people never think that young people have any judgment.[22]

Adams's success in making entry into the newspapers apparently did not occur until 1763, when he began the "Humphrey Ploughjogger" contributions in the humorous dialect anticipatory of Artemus Ward. These began innocently enough in the Boston *Evening Post* in March of that year but extended throughout the summer when he also authored the famous "U." articles on "Private Revenge" and "Self-Delusion" (as Charles Francis Adams labeled them) in the Boston *Gazette*. He had finally achieved some measure of success by carrying on a "dialogue" with himself in several leading papers, as has been remarked. Since he hated to be a "party man" of any kind, he apparently wrote on both sides.[23]

This "dialogue" is particularly revealing. It not only demonstrates an early conservative streak in Adams but shows him to have been of a divided state of mind concerning the nature of man, perhaps because after reading Edmund Burke's *Philosophical Enquiry* and Adam Smith's *Theory of the Moral Sentiments* he was in a philosophical mood, pondering the question, for example, whether we take pleasure in the distresses of others.[24] He also strongly suspects that his best friend at the bar, Jonathan Sewall (who had recently been appointed a Justice of the Peace by the Governor), was the author of the "J." articles which also appear in the *Post* in 1763. These latter writings purported to deal with James Otis, Jr., and with questions then beginning to perturb the Massachusetts political situation. Indeed, Adams's suspicions about Sewall—and we have no other evidence that Sewall was the author of the "J." articles beyond what Adams thought—is similar to his much later suspicion that Sewall was the author of the "Massachusettensis" newspaper articles in 1774. Actually, the Loyalist, Daniel Leonard of Taunton, was the sole author of the latter, although Adams would not believe this until late in life. It is curious that three of Adams's close friends at the bar, and perhaps his closest friends, Leonard, Sewall, and Quincy, all became Loyalists.[25]

The humorous "Ploughjogger" articles in 1763 are, of course, primarily concerned with rural problems, especially with the raising of hemp which the British had recently placed on the "enumerated" list. The subject of such activities had been stimulated by the publication of Jared Eliot's *Essays on Field Husbandry Especially in*

New England, which had been subsidized by Peter Oliver, one of the judges of the Superior Court and a man of whom Adams then had a good opinion.

Some of this anonymous "dialogue" in 1763, however, is concerned with the ideas of crusty old Benjamin Prat, the one-legged Boston lawyer of original mind whom Adams is supposed to have disliked because of his unfriendliness in 1758. Yet Prat's cynical philosophy is quoted with approval in one of the "Ploughjogger" articles. It almost sounds as though John Adams had been carrying on a debate with his old friend and neighbor, Sam Quincy, who had studied law with Prat, as possibly he may have earlier done with Abel Willard in Worcester, who also had studied in Prat's office. Adams must have decided to write up these ideas for the papers. The "dialogue" reveals him to have had a remarkably ambivalent nature, indeed. Resolved not to be a "party" man or to take "sides," he wrote on both sides of the questions which "J." had raised.

It is interesting that Adams was later to speak with considerable respect for Prat, who had headed an antiHutchinson faction in the days of Thomas Pownall, one-time Royal Governor of Massachusetts and a good friend of Americans.[26]

In Adams's "critical years," when he was scribbling all kinds of things in his diary and trying to get into the newspapers, he may sometimes have wondered whether he would ever become a really important lawyer (although such a sentiment would have been out of keeping with his optimistic temper). "Love" had also let him down, and the social life of Braintree could not have seemed quite as bright as it once had been.

Much of this self-doubt was to come to an end in October, 1764, with Adams's marriage to Abigail of nearby Weymouth.[27] In a real love affair, "Lysander" and "Diana" wrote each other ardent letters. However, the brown-eyed girl nine years his junior was not without a mind of her own nor without her own sense of humor, for all of her becoming such a loyal helpmate. She was also a good Whig as well as an advocate of female education, and probably strengthened his own Whiggish, if ambivalent, tendencies. It has even been said that his marriage saved his sanity because he had been exhibiting paranoid (i.e., suspicious) behavior; but whether that was sexual in origin is anybody's guess.

Nabby was also not without having something of gentility in her make-up, being the granddaughter of a Quincy—John Adams always seemed to fall in love with a Quincy—as well as the daughter of an imperious lady of distinguished ministerial lineage, who looked askance at the impetuous young lawyer. Lawyers were still an unknown quantity and Adams had deserted the ministry. The good lady is even said to have managed to hold up the wedding for a time.[28]

Nabby's father, the Reverend Mr. William Smith, seems to have accepted the acquisition of his new son-in-law with Christian fortitude, but for the wedding sermon preached on the text, "And John came neither eating bread nor drinking wine, and ye say, *He hath a devil.*" The Reverend Mr. Smith, who had preached in a similarly humorous vein when his oldest daughter had married Cranch, two years before, was a collector of sayings considered funny in those days. Perhaps he was going to need all the humor he could get, not only having a Quincy for a wife but also a problem son, and a younger daughter with extremely romantic notions and poor judgment.

The long drawn-out engagement finally came to an end. John Adams survived the ordeal of being inoculated for the smallpox in the Boston "pest" house (Abigail's "Momma" especially feared his letters from there would prove contagious). The young folks survived a trip together, and even survived a friend's wish that they marry earlier.[29] They moved to John's house in Braintree where they were to have help both inside and out, and set up housekeeping. They were to be ideally suited to each other for over half a century.

CHAPTER 4

Britannic Statesman

"How easily the People change"

W ITH the conclusion of his "critical years," the ebullient but less humorous John Adams of historical fame begins to appear, i.e., after the Stamp Act Crisis of 1765 and after his marriage to Abigail the year before. His political career was to be interrupted, however, following his courageous defense of the British soldiers in the so-called "Boston Massacre" of 1770, when he fell a prey to misgivings about popular support.[1] He was then to resolve to abandon all politics and to pay full attention to his law practice and to his family,[2] although his public interests were soon resumed.

After 1764 John Adams was a more assertive man—perhaps even a somewhat different one. He naturally saw less of Colonel Josiah Quincy and more of that critical but cautious old Whig, "Grandfather" Colonel John Quincy of Mount Wollaston[3] (who, dying in 1767, had his name bequeathed to his new great-grandson, John Quincy Adams). Even Adams's strictures on Thomas Hutchinson, Chief Justice of the Massachusetts Superior Court and subsequently Governor, are largely a product of this period. Although Hutchinson had been opposed to the Stamp Act, he had preferred to work privately to get it repealed rather than through public resolves or public demonstrations,[4] such as the one which wrecked his house; but his private feelings were not generally known. To persons like John Adams the Stamp Act ushered in a period of "corruption" in which Hutchinson starred; and of course the old suspicions about his friend, Jonathan Sewall, continued, apparently with good reason.[5] After 1764 the distinction between "friends" and "enemies" became increasingly clearer in Adams's mind.

It was never more apparent than in this period how John Adams appeared in the role of "Britannic Statesman" as he has been brilliantly called, i.e., in a "constitutional" sense, for he had only vague ideas about imperial or international affairs.[6] He was concerned, no doubt with Abigail's hearty concurrence, or even encouragement, lest old British constitutional rights be impaired in America. There it apparently had its only hope, an idea which all English liberals had publicly and privately supported. Indeed, an Englishman, Thomas Hollis, a supporter of the "Old Whig" point of view, had for years been sending books on the subject of "liberty" to sundry Americans.

Much of Adams's feeling probably was a part of a nascent American nationalism for home rule. He had expressed such feelings as early as The Great War for The Empire ("The French and Indian War"), although he had then favored American colonial union only to produce a better Empire.

Practical politics had meantime come to his astonished attention. In February, 1763, he had learned of a certain "Caucas Clubb" which was said to determine elections at the Boston town meeting.[7]

The Stamp Act led the ever scribbling Adams to write a series of unsigned articles for the Boston *Gazette*. He also composed resolutions of protest for a Braintree town meeting which he initiated, and which in turn was to influence other towns, although it is sad to relate that Braintree then ungenerously refused to send him to the General Court.[8] The ideas for the articles had originally been discussed by Adams for the benefit of a "sodality," or club, which Jeremiah Gridley had recently organized in Boston for certain lawyers. These articles were promptly published in England through the interest of Thomas Hollis, under the title *A Dissertation on the Canon and Feudal Law,* although without Adams's knowledge. Indeed, he was even to pay scant attention to them in his *Autobiography,* perhaps because they were to be thrown in his teeth in later years.

The *Dissertation* argued that Europe had produced a combination of tyrannies unacceptable in America. Of feudal tyranny little was said, but there was much about religion, much of it anti-Romish. The first Puritans were said to have fled England to escape religious tyranny. Let the pulpits resound with doctrines of religious liberty, Adams stormed. Timidity and ignorance were both weaknesses, he said. "People" were a "balance" in government, but he really held the old Puritan vision that a pure and chosen America should shine forth as a beacon to the Old World. His real target, of course, was the "unconstitutional" Stamp Act itself.[9]

Adams always was to consider the real cause of the American Revolution to be the issuing of such "unconstitutional" acts by Parliament. Some of these ideas he expressed in his "Clarendon" articles in the *Gazette* in 1766, for he continued to love to write anonymously for the press. It is curious that he should have used an old Royalist name, even if Clarendon had become an exile. Purporting to be the shade of the Earl he answered a certain "William Pym," who had warned of the power of Parliament over colonial charters. Adams replied on the grounds of constitutionality, as did James Otis, Jr. over the signature of "Hampden." Adams also attacked "Pym's" "counterfeited humanity" and his "problematical" integrity in the old Royalist struggle of the seventeenth century. "Clarendon" applauded the Americans for their spirited defense of the British constitution in the eighteenth century and said that he would now "scarcely" even call the protectorate of Cromwell a "usurpation." Despite all of Adams's emphasis on "liberty," the "Clarendon" essays show his early intimation that a "mixed" form of government distinguished the English in legislative matters at least. He asserted that all English liberties go back to Saxon times and that "all men are born equal."[10] Presumably its benefits were to apply to Englishmen everywhere, certainly in America.

Meantime the famous Stamp Act Congress had met in New York City with nine colonies represented, under the chairmanship of a Massachusetts man who refused to sign its final resolves and later became a Loyalist. Its resolutions, probably drafted originally by William Samuel Johnson of Connecticut, a one-time colonial agent in England and subsequently a "neutral," were, however, conservative. They argued that the Stamp Act was unconstitutional primarily because the colonists were too far away to be properly represented in Parliament, and that there could be "no taxation without representation." This was more or less the argument which had been popularized by Daniel Dulany, Jr. of Maryland, later also a "neutral."

These years are those of the enthusiasm of the "Liberty Boys," one of whose leaders was Benjamin Edes, the printer of the Boston *Gazette*. In that paper, in January and February of 1767, John Adams had answered an administration defense in his anonymous "Governor Winthrop to Governor Bradford" replies to "Philanthrop," i.e., his old friend Sewall, whom he called not only "contemptible" but "abominable." The quarrel was really over Governor Bernard's refusal to permit the House of Representatives to administer the oath to members from Newburyport whose representation was twice what the Governor considered proper. The Governor had reluctantly (against his Instructions) permitted the town of Newburyport to be divided providing that it should not increase its representation. The *Gazette* hailed one of Adams's replies as a "delicious regalement for the benefit of all lovers of their country." Adams, anonymously of course, accused "Philanthrop" of trying to arouse her enemies by attacking liberty in the manner of the Stuart kings, i.e., by denying the right of the House to pass on its own members. "The only question is, who shall judge?"[11]

Despite such political controversy and his love of writing, John Adams continued to pursue his career as a lawyer, eventually becoming one of the important legal figures of the Province. He even took on two law clerks in 1769 and his library continued to grow. How good a trial lawyer he was we simply do not know; the old story that the way to beat him in court was to make him lose his temper may have referred to the bellicose temper he undoubtedly had, or it may be nothing but political gossip.

His real success in the law came gradually despite all his learning and his advantageous marriage. It was not really until about 1768 that he entered upon the most active phase of his career. One of his most prestigious clients in those years was the Kennebeck Company of Falmouth, in Casco Bay, Maine, which paid him thirty pounds a trip to cover fees and expenses for the trip Eastward.[12] This also involved Adams in a number of "mast" controversies with his old classmate, John Wentworth of New Hampshire, the last Royal Governor of that Province, who was the Surveyor of the King's Woods in those parts.

Adams's frequent law journeys on horseback were now more than ever a part of his life. Circuit riding included attending Inferior and Superior Court sessions in Springfield, Worcester, Plymouth, Salem, and even Falmouth, Maine. His cases also necessitated frequent appearances in Boston at the Vice Admiralty courts and the Supreme Court of Probate. Matters involved all kinds of things, such as divorce, wills, rape, and trespass, and frequently had to do with the Common Law. Adams usually appeared for the plaintiffs, but these were drawn from all ranks of society. For example, late in his career he appeared at the Falmouth Inferior Court as one of the advocates of the merchant Richard King of Scarborough, Maine, whose mansion had been destroyed in 1766 and who claimed to have suffered subsequent vandalism. King's house was said to have been destroyed originally because he had got his estate "by robbing the poor" and deserved to be whipped and to have his ears cut off. Adams's appeal to the jury was highly emotional: he spoke of "The Cruelty, the Terror, the Horror of the whole dismal scene." It must have had but limited effect, however: one of the alleged culprits was found not guilty in a parallel case and was even given compensation out of what Adams had won for King.[13]

It was in connection with the King affair that Adams wrote his wife, "These private Mobs, I do and will detest." Popular commotions could be justified only when "Fundamentals" were involved. "But these Tarrings and Featherings . . . by . . . Rabbles cannot even be excused. . . ."[14]

Unfortunately, the diary, or journal, entries tell little about John Adams in these years, especially between 1766 and 1770. Perhaps he was becoming a little cynical, as when he noted in 1767 that "Suits generally Spring from Passion"; or perhaps the press of legal business was simply becoming too great. Only occasionally does he become truly philosophical. "To what object, are my Views directed? What is the End and Purpose of my Studies, Journeys, Labours of all Kinds of Body and Mind, of Tongue and Pen? Am I grasping at Money, or Scheming for Power? Am I planning the Illustration of my Family or the Welfare of my Country? These are great Questions." He complains about the stress he is undergoing. "In Truth, I am tossed about so much, from Post to Pillar, that I have not Leisure and Tranquillity enough, to consider distinctly my own Views, Objects and Feelings."[15]

Politics simply would not keep out of John Adams's thinking. He wrote his sister-in-law in January, 1767 (perhaps trying to reassure her), that he cared little for "News Paper Politics," and had been at peace for eight months; but this was a deliberate blind. He was even then writing anonymously for the *Gazette,* answering "Philanthrop."[16]

Constitutional principles never could be forgotten. Even when he defended poor Otis in 1771 it probably was because Otis still retained something of the aura of "Britannic Statesman" like himself, even if Otis had differed from him about the power of Parliament. Problems of self-interest were also always present. In 1768, Adams's *Autobiography* tells us, he ("Old Swim or Sink") refused Jonathan Sewall's offer to make him Advocate General of the Court of Admiralty at the Governor's instigation, on Thomas Hutchinson's recommendation and regardless of his political principles. However, Hutchinson in his *History* says that Adams, not knowing what side to take, was refused being made a Justice of the Peace because he had offended the Governor; but perhaps both things were true at different times.[17]

A new political stimulus had arisen in 1768, when the enthusiasm of the "Liberty Boys" (of whom Adams was not one) was revived against the "Townshend Duty Acts." These were proposals to raise taxes in America 'indirectly,' as Benjamin Franklin had once told Parliament the Americans apparently meant. The "Sons" now tried to reimpose commercial nonimportation as a means of combating this new iniquity. The Duty Acts were accompanied by British troops being brought to Boston to combat the action of mobs and to preserve the peace, and bringing with them, no doubt, their patronage at "Mt. Whoredom" and other red light places to the scandal of all proper Bostonians.

Adams discussed these matters in the "Instructions of the Town of Boston" in 1768 and 1769.[18] In the first of these he hinted of rumors about troops being brought to Boston "to dragoon us into passive obedience," and in the second, it was stated as a fact. There had been rejoicing in America when the Stamp Act had been repealed, he said, but acts of the Royal navy and customs officials were now resulting in the seizing of vessels (such as the sloop *Liberty* of John Hancock, for whom Adams was then attorney) with the full approval of the American Board of Commissioners. Such was the "miserable case of North America." An exception was being made between the English subject in Great Britain and the English subject in America, he said. Revenues collected by the vice admiralty courts in America could be recovered with the approval of a single judge, whereas they could be recovered in Britain only by jury trial.[19]

The presence of British soldiers in Boston resulted in several episodes, the most famous being that of March 5, 1770, the so-called "Boston Massacre." As one of the counsel for the defense of the British officer and his men, who were in danger of not receiving a fair trial, John Adams never showed off to better advantage. It revealed his innate conscience, and perhaps his ambivalence, because of his recognition of the necessity for keeping the bar independent and impartial. Of course the Boston *Gazette* resented the outcome which was more or less a victory for John Adams and his associates (whereas Hutchinson thought that Adams had been willing to sacrifice his clients' interest to the feelings of the Town, perhaps a sour afterthought encouraged by Loyalists).[20]

Unfortunately, following his courageous defense of the British soldiers in 1770, outspoken but now middle-aged John Adams had a letdown. He had always disliked the air in Boston, a place he had thought "dirty" and "noisy," and his health had suffered. Popular opinion seemed to have deserted him even if support by the Patriot leaders had not. The narrowminded farmers close to the Boston market were like a lot of "peasants," he scornfully said.[21] Adams moved his family back to his Braintree farm early in 1771 but kept his Boston law office despite his antiBoston feelings, and sought to recover his health by taking a long horseback ride over the mountains into the Connecticut River Valley, drinking the mineral waters at Stafford Springs on the way. His vanity as well as his health had suffered and a new pessimism had entered his soul. He wrote in his diary, "How easily the People change, and give up their Friends and their Interest," and that he was "left alone, in the World." He longed to get back to his farm and family.[22]

Perhaps because of this brief letdown John Adams was not active in the Boston Committee of Correspondence. Cousin Samuel Adams, the successor to James Otis, Jr. (who is said to have been acting erratically but who is also said to have feared Sam Adams), had organized this in 1772, with the approval of the Boston town meeting.[23] This had encouraged similar town actions throughout the Province which in turn had occasioned Governor Hutchinson's address to the General Court in January, 1773, arguing the necessity for Parliamentary authority. In the House reply, John Adams played some kind of role.

Nevertheless, as shown in his notes for an oration for the Town of Braintree in 1772, John Adams was now primarily concerned with the "science" of government. While arguing that all kingdoms had once been free and that it was the rights of "Us the People" that were being invaded, he still believed that the best kind of government was "mixed." This referred to a mixture of monarchy, aristocracy, and democracy.[24] Henceforth he seems to have emphasized more than ever the necessity for the proper organization of government, rather than for a mere reliance on popular consistency. The old problem of human nature which the "Ploughjogger" articles had raised back in 1763 (and human nature was ever his stumbling block), seems never to have been completely settled in his mind. His law practice may have had something to do with this attitude.

There seemed to be a lull in Massachusetts's politics in 1772. Governor Hutchinson was becoming popular again. Even Otis now ranted against John Adams, alleging his lack of "heart" for military matters and his love of money, to which John Adams in his diary, in characteristic fashion, poured out his spleen on poor Otis for having used politics for reasons of family nepotism.[25] Adams even refused to prepare an oration in memory of the "Boston Massacre" lest he be exposed—amongst other things—to what he called the "malicious tongues on both Sides of the Question."[26]

Perhaps John Adams in 1772 was retreating to his old love of books in analyzing what really constitutes sound government. There had always been something "bookish" about his thinking, which was an overly simplified "Whig" version of history. Like so many of the ideas of his fellows, and even of Tom Paine who cherished a life-long hatred for William the Conqueror, some of these ideas sound today like an early version of *Ivanhoe*.[27]

For whatever reason—his ambition, his enemies always charged— Adams was soon aroused, like an old war-horse, first by an old threat and then by a new one. Almost simultaneously with his contribution to the House reply to Governor Hutchinson's insistence on Parliamentary authority, he was faced with a legal question which had "constitutional" overtones, i.e., the independency of the judiciary. A proposal that judges' salaries henceforth be paid by the Crown was the subject of his dispute with a fellow lawyer and former Whig, General William Brattle. To the latter the new proposal did not undermine the independency of the judges but to Adams it did, and he characteristically drew on his learning to prove the point. His communications to the *Gazette* continued long after Brattle, perhaps worn out, had given up the argument.

In his *Autobiography* John Adams was to boast that his legal principles in this dispute had subsequently become "almost universally prevalent among the People of America." He then feared, however, that under the Jefferson administration these principles were in danger of being lost because all liberty seemed to be at the mercy of "a Majority and of a tryumphant Party."[28] Party spirit and mobs he had always despised, but "the cause of my Country" had always seemed to him to be a very different thing. He had been ahead of his time in acting like a Britannic statesman before the American Revolution occurred while simultaneously being an ardent nationalist; which is another way of saying that while undoubtedly ebullient and ambitious, John Adams was also ambivalent in character.

CHAPTER 5

The Continental Congress

"Politics I cant write, in Honour"

JOHN Adams's occasional diary entries continue to be revealing as to his innermost feelings in the 1770's, although it does not follow that his outward performance always conformed to these. He had long ago decided that "dissimulation" or "concealment" might be a necessary part of prudence in religious or political matters.[1]

The year 1773, especially scanty for diary entries, was truly an *annus mirabilis.* It aroused Adams from his political lethargy and added to his hatred of Thomas Hutchinson. The year had begun with the reply of the House to the Governor and with Adams's legal controversy with Brattle, but the revelation of Hutchinson's and others' letters in March led him to condemn all such persons as "deliberate Villains" who were "ambitious and avaricious." The Boston Tea Party in December was "magnificent" and showed "Sublimity," and might result in the death of some of the government faction, beneficially in several cases, he thought.[2] The "Party" had been made possible apparently by the Boston Committee of Correspondence under the wily influence of cousin Samuel Adams, but in this action John Adams himself had played no part.[3]

Indeed, John Adams never was a member of any Committee of Correspondence[4] and apparently always remained ignorant of cousin Sam Adams's arrangements. Perhaps John Adams never did really understand what was going on.

Despite his later claim to have furnished the evidence for the Massachusetts House of Representatives to prepare a bill of indictment for the impeachment of Chief Justice Peter Oliver (who had succeeded his brother, the one-time Stamp Act collector), there is little evidence for this in John Adams's diary and none at all in the

family letters. Adams had formerly admired Peter Oliver, personally.
The impeachment preceedings must nevertheless have added fuel to
the fires of popular resentment in Yankee land. Governor Hutchinson, in disgust, was to leave for England the following year and Oliver
was even to be afraid to attend his own brother's funeral.

The "Tea Party" had resulted, as John Adams had feared and
expected, in the "Intolerable Acts" by the British Parliament in 1774,
i.e., the closing of the Port of Boston until the tea should be paid for,
the Regulating Act which changed the nature of the Massachusetts
government, and the Quebec Act which extended the boundaries of
that Province and which seemed to favor Catholics by extending
freedom of religion. Boston was to be governed by a military man
acting as Governor, General Thomas Gage, the Commander-in-
Chief; and although "Tommy" was to try to be a tactful man, much
criticized even by his own officers for leaning backwards in protecting
citizens,[5] he was to be considered something of a "monster" by the
Patriots.

Feelings sometimes ran intense for personal as well as for public
reasons. As John wrote Abigail in July, "I will not willingly see
Blockheads, whom I have a Right to despise, elevated above me, and
insolently triumphing over me." His motives had always been pure,
he apparently thought, even if those of others were not. Printers, in
particular, were "hot, indiscreet Men." His newspaper scribbling had
always "religiously and punctiliously" avoided personal reflections;
but writing by other people was apparently another matter.[6]

In the summer of 1774, having again transferred his family to
Braintree, John prepared to represent Massachusetts in a general
meeting, or "Congress," in Philadelphia. Samuel Adams, Thomas
Cushing, and Robert Treat Paine were to accompany him; a fifth
delegate found it impossible to go. Five hundred pounds was
provided for their expenses which John said would be great, although
he also wrote Abigail that the "public Good" would be their only
reward.[7] The delegates obviously were to try to convince representatives from other colonies that the crisis in Massachusetts was now the
concern of all.

Sympathy for the people of Boston was widespread and the
Congress seems to have been the result of a general idea. The Virginia
Burgesses, in rump session in May, had favored a united meeting, and
so had Committees of Correspondence in Rhode Island and New
York. In the latter, "conservatives" had also suggested the idea. The
Massachusetts House of Representatives on June 27 had resolved

that a meeting of committees was "highly expedient and necessary," and had suggested Philadelphia as the place on September 1. Other colonies followed, but the "radicals"—those bent on extreme measures, i.e., members of the "violent party," as Galloway was to term them—chiefly engineered the event in various ways rather than through regular Colonial assemblies. The purposes of the Congress were not revolutionary but rather a redress of grievances and the protection of "liberty." While clearly nationalistic, the Congress was to seek a restoration of "harmony and union" between Great Britain and the colonies. Such were the instructions of most of the delegates.[8]

John Adams's picturesque diary account of the trip to Philadelphia in August, 1774, is a much fuller account than usual. Whigs all along the way, including Silas Deane in Connecticut, encouraged the Massachusetts delegates; and the description of all persons encountered, even in New York City, is priceless. The hospitality of Philadelphians abounded and John Adams especially liked their beer, although he had heard that the washing of clothes was not as well done there or in New York as in Boston. He eventually also was to conclude that morals and manners in Philadelphia were not as pure as those at home.[9]

The real question at Philadelphia from the beginning was, who would control the Congress: the moderates who favored reconciliation or the radicals who wanted extreme measures? Even moderates, especially Pennsylvania's Speaker, Joseph Galloway, were concerned about American "rights," but they also wanted to save the Empire with a restoration of "union and harmony" so as to bring about "welfare and happiness." Pennsylvanians like New Yorkers and a delegate from South Carolina feared too much resistance. The first, John Adams thought, were unduly sensitive on the issue of religious liberty as advanced by the "Broadbrims," or Quakers (whom he always disliked), and by some New England Baptists.[10]

The Congress was composed of a number of remarkable men with varying degrees of political experience, and although John Dickinson was later to consider its attitude as having been "conciliatory," the radicals had it all their own way. Even the selection of Carpenters Hall as a meeting place, instead of the State House as suggested by Speaker Galloway, had politics in it. So did the election of its Secretary, Charles Thomson, the "Sam Adams" of the City of Brotherly Love. Like the well known John Dickinson, who was originally kept out of the Congress, Thomson was a bitter foe of Galloway.

Almost as soon as the Congress met it heard the horrid news of
"War! War! War!" because of a "bombardment" of Boston, and
although this report proved to be false news, it gave the radicals an
eventual advantage.[11] On September 17 the Congress wholeheart-
edly endorsed the "Suffolk Resolves" of Suffolk County, Massachusetts, which breathed determined resistance to all British rule in
Boston and Massachusetts and which Paul Revere had just ridden
into town to report.[12] Sam Adams may have had a hand in preparing
the Resolves since he is said to have kept the dispatches warm.

The most fateful decision of the Congress came on September 28
with the rejection by the vote of a single colony of the plan of union
submitted by Joseph Galloway, based on the old Albany Plan of
Benjamin Franklin, formerly a political ally of Galloway. It combined the idea of an American Assembly within the British Empire,
i.e., an "imperial" solution for American rights. All reference to the
Galloway proposal was subsequently expunged from the records of
the Congress, however, and the plan is almost forgotten by American
history. It is also never mentioned in John Adams's letters, although
his diary does give extracts of Galloway's speech. "But Politics I cant
write, in Honour," as he had earlier said.[13] The suppression of the
vote on the Galloway Plan has been called by one scholar "a striking
example of what a later generation was to call managed news," and
another scholar has referred to its rejection as the "one great negative
fact" in the work of a notable assembly.[14]

Galloway, unfortunately, while believing in American rights did
not believe that such rights came from "nature," thus apparently
differing from John Adams, although the latter tells us in his
Autobiography that the idea was retained as a "Resource" to which
the members might eventually be driven. Galloway subsequently
turned into something of a recluse and even a sulky person, as well as
a badly menaced one.[15] He was to become one of the most famous of
the Loyalists, like that Episcopalian preacher who had given such an
eloquent prayer for the Congress in its opening session on suggestion
of that old "Puritan Saint," Sam Adams, who declared that he (i.e.
Sam Adams) was no bigot in religious matters.

The delegates proudly affirmed their rights as Englishmen, as they
adopted a Declaration of Rights and Grievances derived from "the
immutable laws of nature, the principles of the English constitution,
and the several charters or compacts." They also drew up a petition to
their "Most Gracious Sovereign," King George III, made an appeal
to the British people, and established a nonintercourse Association to

prohibit any further trade with England, except for the exportation of rice and indigo which the delegates from South Carolina insisted upon. Should a redress of grievances not be obtained (something which seemed to have been anticipated and in any case was a very vague thing), a second Congress was to meet in May of the following year. The Congress adjourned on October 26 and a happy John Adams returned home.

During the six months which followed, Whig committees made life miserable for all moderates in the enforcement of the Association. Tarring and feathering became widespread. "Luxury" activities, like horseracing and the giving of balls, were also frowned upon. The pressure of public opinion must have been immense since all offenders were reported to the press. The Congress had made this possible by recommending that committees be set up in "every county, city, and town." As one bitter "conservative" put it (the future Bishop Seabury), it was better to suffer "enslavement" by a king than by zealous committeemen whom he compared to rats and vermin.[16]

As a New England man John Adams no doubt continued to remain more or less happy in this period, even after hearing the news that George III had declared the New England governments to be in a state of rebellion. If Pandora's Box had been opened, Adams did not know it. The Association especially rankled England, where despite a gesture by Lord North even old friends of America like Pitt, Burke, and Barre were convinced that Parliamentary authority in the Empire had to be maintained.

Perhaps, as Abigail Adams in February, 1775, wrote Mercy Otis Warren, that ardent feminist and budding authoress whose *The Group* had been published in the Boston *Gazette* in January (through the interest of John Adams), the only recourse was now to arms. Abigail wrote as an outraged Yankee.[17]

Unfortunately, for these months there is a gap in John Adams's diary and little information in the letters. Even the "battle" of Lexington and Concord in April does not appear, although Abigail's irresponsible brother seems somehow to have been involved.[18] One is forced to emulate Charles Francis Adams and to refer to John Adams's *Autobiography,* written in old age:[19]

Upon our Return to Massachusetts, I found myself elected by the Town of Braintree into the provincial Congress, and attended that Service as long as it sat. About this time, Drapers Paper in Boston swarmed with Writers, and among an immense quantity of meaner productions appeared a Writer under the Signature of Massachusettensis, suspected but never that I knew ascertained to be written by two of my old Friends Jonathan Sewall and Daniel Leonard. [Actually by Leonard.] These Papers were well written, abounded with Wit, discovered good Information, and were conducted with a Sublety of Art and Address, wonderfully calculated to keep Up the Spirits of their Party, to depress ours, to spread intimidation and to make Proselytes among those, whose Principles and Judgment give Way to their fears, and these comprise at least one third of Mankind. Week after Week passed away, and these Papers made a very visible impression on many Minds. No Answer appeared, and indeed, some who were capable, were too busy and others too timorous. I began at length to think seriously of the Consequences and began to write, under the Signature of Novanglus, and continued every Week, in the Boston Gazette, till the 19th. of April. . . . the battle of Lexington on the 19th of April, changed the Instruments of Warfare from the Penn to the Sword.

The importance of the opinions advanced by "Massachusettensis" and "Novanglus" are here properly emphasized; and an extract of the latter was immediately published in London by J. Almon. The controversy marked the beginning of the end so far as "imperial" relations were concerned. In addition to making continuing and scornful references to "Tories," Adams underscored what Thomas Jefferson of Virginia had recently asserted in his *Summary View:* that America was not really a part of the British Empire at all, having always been outside the "realm." The only tie now recognized by "Whigs" connecting America with Old England was that of allegiance to the King, and John Adams made it clear that such allegiance was due the latter only in his "natural" person.[20]

The issue after April, 1775, was clearly one of war, or the preparation for it, and Adams's feelings were strengthened after the Battle of "Bunker Hill" in June. All fear of popular displeasure, and his old sense of humor, had completely evaporated. Still not a "party man," he was an ardent patriot. Of Loyalists, as such, he seems to have been unaware. There were many "ministerial men" and "trimmers," but they were all "Tories," i.e., unpatriotic men, according to Adams.

There is no record in the Adams diary of the Second Continental Congress beginning in Philadelphia in May, 1775, except for the record of expenses he kept. Adams was in a poor state of health in Philadelphia that spring, disliked the climate, and complained about the caprice of certain of his associates; but he was correct when he wrote Abigail that "The Congress will support the Massachusetts."[21]

Whig enthusiasm was apparent even in the middle states, which had always been the chief stumbling block. There, too, a new sense of radicalism seemed to be emerging. The idea of reconciliation with Britain was rapidly fading.

Adams proposed Washington as Commander-in-Chief of a newly-formed Continental army in June, thus alienating John Hancock who aspired to that position, and only with disgust signed an "Olive Branch" petition to the King. A "Declaration of Reasons for Appealing to Arms," eloquently written by that moderate Whig, John Dickinson, seemed pointless to Radicals.[22]

For the "third" session of the Congress, beginning in September, 1775, the diary accounts resume; and Adams's dislike of Dickinson and his embarrassment because of an intercepted letter of his which reflected poorly on Dickinson (and amused and angered the British) began to emerge.[23] His thoughts also surfaced that the radical Lees of Virginia were all "sensible," and that men like Samuel Chase of Maryland were really admirable. Much of the work of the Congress had to do with military supplies and the prospects for establishing a navy. He served on numerous committees.

When visiting home in 1775, John Adams was to recall in old age, he had been appalled to learn that some people had come to think the absence of courts of law a very good thing; and he had begun to wonder whether debts and debtors were not the real goal of patriotic activity. He later denied that he had then known of the enormous debts which Virginians and others owed abroad, i.e., before the Revolution.[24]

The idea of a complete revolution taking place in American society seemed to Adams to make no sense, even in 1776. True, he wanted a pure republic to emerge, a "city set upon a hill" in the biblical phrase of the Puritans, but he would have had the suffrage issue, for example, left alone. Rumors that revolution encouraged all kinds of insubordination, by slaves, Indians, apprentices, women, etc., were merely Tory propaganda in his opinion. Only the possession of property, preferably small amounts of land, ever gave men any sense of judgment, he thought. The suffrage might be extended, admittedly, but this logically might include children as well as women. Abigail teased him about this and accused his sex of being tyrannical, but she seems to have acquiesced like any good eighteenth-century wife.[25]

John Adams believed that the idea of organization, i.e., of machinery, necessarily came first, whether in political or military matters.

Perhaps this is what led him to question some of Tom Paine's ideas in the latter's immensely popular *Common Sense,* which that recent arrival from England had published early in 1776. Paine wrote in a "manly" style, as Adams said, but he was essentially a "tearer-down" rather than a "builder-up" or architect where political institutions were concerned.

One reason for Adams writing his own *Thoughts on Government* that year was to conteract this lack in Paine—it really was an addendum to Paine whose pamphlet was sometimes being credited to Adams.[26]

The *Thoughts* was a product of John Adams's life-long belief in the "science" and balance of government. It was intended to assist the states that were emerging out of the old colonies, especially in the South. There seemed to Adams to be a dangerous tendency towards too much simplicity in government. Checks and balances would always be necessary as well as bicameral legislatures. Tyranny eternally threatened, he thought, when mutually opposing elements were not provided for. The happiness of most of the people was always to be aimed at and only a republican government could do this; but only the proper organization of even a republic could make it work. The legislative power still had to be dual despite the need for popular representation. Of course, underlying all of this, Adams reasoned, was the need for education and morality such as the "Yankees" had always known, but which he did not mention.[27]

The moderation of the middle states having been broken especially by Whig efforts in Pennsylvania,[28] Adams became an outspoken antagonist for independence in the Congress of 1776. He was a brave, resolute, and pugnacious figure, as well as a most learned one. The dogs of war had finally been unleashed, and Abigail was as Whiggish as himself. How fortunate he had been, he tells us in his *Autobiography,* to have had such a wife at such a time, and to have had support at home. Had his relatives been like John Dickinson's wife and mother, subject to Quaker principles (he later said that he had heard), there would have been a continual torrent of criticism and warnings about his being hanged.[29] Adams stuck to his goals despite all of his family troubles. A wave of distemper had swept Eastern Massachusetts in 1775 and had given Abigail a terrible time. Even young brother Elihu had died, presumably from camp dysentery,[30] having held a minor commission secured through John Adams's influence and apparently despite his mother's opposition.[31] Abigail had lost her own mother several years before, and was now being given the "pox."

The family health record was appalling, but the work of revolution had to go on.

The strain of the times made John Adams even more waspish than usual in his comments upon men and measures in 1776. In the Congress, which had now become a regular thing, he still had to fight occasionally against sectionalist feeling against New England. The King's refusing to protect all his subjects in America had forfeited all allegiance, in Adams's opinion. Of course the middle colonies were still reluctant about independence, and even some Southerners had begun to wonder at the lengths to which things were going. Timid persons like Dickinson who continued to hope for concessions from Britain appeared a hindrance, for they continued to appeal to reason when independence was demanded.

The influence of *Common Sense* and the action of Whig committeemen everywhere had nevertheless been great, and public opinion had become a real factor, so that radicals in Congress continued to hold the upper hand. A resolution had been accepted in April that each colony form a new government, ports had been thrown open to world trade except with Britain, and there was soon to be a Declaration of Independence. Fortunately, old Benjamin Franklin, who, disgusted, had returned from England, backed radicals to the limit.[32]

John Adams was truly the "Atlas" of independence in 1776. A member of the committee to formulate a Declaration of Independence—largely the work of its gifted chairman, Thomas Jefferson of Virginia, who had acquired the reputation of being a good writer—Adams was the principal defender of that Declaration on the floor of Congress. (Jefferson would have been poor in such a role ever disliking public speaking.) It is regrettable that Adams's speech on that occasion has not been preserved. If a third of all the people (although they did not dare confess it), and a majority of people in the middle states really "detested" the Declaration in their hearts, as he later said,[33] he presumably ignored this attitude at the time in the name of expediency. All important measures are carried by narrow margins, he once observed.

The independence of the "United States" was promptly followed by a discussion of the organization of a new central government, which some conservatives thought should have come first. In this, Adams's old antagonist, John Dickinson of Delaware, was to play a leading role, drafting the original plan of confederation which Congress debated for a year; but Dickinson had suffered a serious setback. Like all of his kind, he had fallen "like Grass before the Scythe." Despite Dickinson's later service as a soldier, even at Valley Forge, he remains something of a dim figure in American history.[34]

It was not so with triumphant John Adams, no longer just a "Yankee." Throughout the remainder of 1776 and most of 1777 he did a vast amount of work for the Congress during most difficult years. He even criticized Washington and is said to have been jealous of him; but it should be remembered that Adams had headed up the Congressional Committee on Ordnance, was Chairman of its Board of War, and always studied books on military matters.

In November, 1777, John Adams finally left the Congress to return to his home and law practice. But his record was not forgotten; nor was his "inflexible integrity" forgotten. He was almost immediately appointed by the Congress in "room" of Silas Deane to be an American Commissioner to the Court of France.[35] An entirely new phase of his career and education was to begin. Presumably, it was to have something to do with honesty.

CHAPTER 6

Mostly Abroad

"What a pretty Thing it is to be an American Minister"

SINCE John Adams had the reputation of being an honest man, and since Silas Deane was to be treated by Congress as though he were not, the issue of honesty was raised when Adams was appointed in 1777 in "room" of Deane as a Commissioner to France.[1] There was to be an enlargement of that word's meaning, however, when even John Adams found that things abroad were not quite as simple as they seemed at home.

Perhaps the foreign policy of the United States from that day to this may be summed up in some such way, i.e., that things abroad are never quite as simple as they seem.

When John Adams approached Bordeaux in late March, 1778, he must have been stunned, one supposes, to learn that the American Commissioners, encouraged by a desperate Congress, had made a perpetual political alliance with France predicated upon her going to war with England. They had also made a treaty of commerce and friendship. John Adams, who now saw his trip as useless, did not object to the Alliance (the only one ever made in our history prior to N.A.T.O., by the way). Indeed, he praised it on several occasions, though he seems to have ignored it pretty largely in his diary. The Alliance with France clearly saved American independence, but one would have expected Adams to have said something critical at first. There were European implications in the Alliance because of territorial questions in the New World, problems that were to embarrass him as President twenty years later,[2] and it ran contrary to his basic philosophy.

The background is very important. John Adams had been on a Congressional committee in 1776 to draw up a model treaty for use in foreign affairs. Alliances to Adams, then at least, had meant not political agreements but only commercial and navigation agreements. Commerce with the thirteen colonies, long a monopoly of England, was sure to be snatched at by the French, he assumed. Such American Revolutionary thought had been greatly influenced by the French, especially by the "enlightened" eighteenth century *philosophes*. Republican simplicity should prevail in foreign as well as in domestic matters, they had taught; conventional diplomacy and cynical "balance of power" politics were to be a thing of the past.[3]

Adams had not only agreed with this thinking originally, but had even once contemplated the interdependence of all revolutionary ideals, i.e., independence, confederation, and foreign aid, in something like a spirit of isolation. Tom Paine had viewed them similarly in *Common Sense:* European ways being wicked, alliances involving Americans in European conflicts were at all costs to be avoided. In late 1778, therefore, Adams would seem to have done something like an about-face.[4]

Perhaps Adams's old ambivalence, or pragmatism, was merely coming out again and he was being merely opportunistic. After all, England remained the true enemy. "I never had so much trouble in my life as here," he once complained, but what he really meant was that no matter if France in many ways agreed with him and made him fat, he was always being given an antiFrench reputation because of British propaganda.[5]

After the Alliance, French aid to America could be given officially, having here-to-fore been done unofficially (which had been a part of Deane's trouble). Being in France did give Adams the chance to see just how intimate relations with an allied foreign power might work. It also gave him a chance to become acquainted with Le Comte de Vergennes, whom he finally got around to seeing, the French foreign minister, an old-style diplomat. Vergennes had been foremost in favoring aid for America and for seeking its independence, but he was primarily interested in having international revenge at the expense of England, and sometimes preferred to honor Spanish claims before those by Americans.[6]

Much of John Adams's time in France was taken up by involvement in the endless quarrels between the remaining American commissioners, especially between Arthur Lee and Franklin. Although Adams was impartial he naturally sided with Lee, a brother of that Richard Henry Lee of Virginia, an old radical ally in Congress. The difficulties between the commissioners had also been occasioned by carelessness in the accounts of Silas Deane, in those informal days of 1776 and 1777 when everything in France had been secret. Although Adams was once to acknowledge Deane's great aid in getting military supplies to America when things there had earlier looked so bad, he now sided with Lee in the latter's suspicions of Deane, and in the 1779 Congressional investigation of Deane's activities. Not the least of the charges against Deane was that he had been venal as well as careless. All of the Lees seem to have had more than their fair share of suspicions about their fellow men, and all were dead set against anyone making money out of the Revolution—as Deane apparently was trying to do. Adams, equally adamant, also had his share of suspicions about people.

He was even becoming increasingly suspicious of old Dr. Franklin, who with the others had so clearly saved American independence with the Alliance, but who got along so well with the French, liked their ladies so much, and prided himself on his homely French speaking ability being so good. Dr. Franklin may have been a great genius but he was surely not a great moralist in practice, in Adams's opinion. That the good Doctor came to appear as something of a moral disgrace, Adams was to emphasize in no uncertain terms in his characterization of Franklin in his *Autobiography*.[7]

It was fortunate that John Adams's eldest son, eleven-year-old John Quincy Adams, accompanied him on the perilous trip to France. Again and again he refers to the boy's company and how much it meant to him, although the boy's expenses at school (he was there with a son of Silas Deane, and a grandson of Franklin) were items to be considered. The father's use of the French language showed up badly alongside that of his son—the boy seemed to learn so much faster. The father did chat, however, with everyone he could, especially with shopkeepers and with people at taverns, had read Molière when coming over, and had gone to the theater, script in hand, whenever possible.[8]

Provincial John Adams apparently liked many things about the French despite his uneasiness about their religion and morals; his diary is studded with references to the many affairs he attended in Paris. He returned home in July, 1779, on a French frigate, *La Sensible,* having been courted and praised in leaving; but so had poor Deane, the year before.

Arriving back in Boston in August, "Mr. Roundface" (as the unfriendly John Paul Jones called him)[9] only had time to see Abigail and the children before attending in September a constitutional convention in Cambridge, as the delegate from Braintree. This convention was to give the people of Massachusetts a new constitution—perhaps the most famous of all Revolutionary state constitutions. An earlier proposal had been rejected by the Massachusetts people in 1778, perhaps because they had read too much Tom Paine and agreed with him that all government was a badge of lost innocence. They were also to show signs of apathy in 1780 when asked to ratify the new document.

As the most active member of a subcommittee of a larger committee on policy, John Adams was the "principal Engineer" of the Massachusetts Constitution of 1780.[10] Changes were subsequently made in his original report; a prime example, of course, is the substitution of men being born "free and equal" in place of their being "born equally free and independent," as Adams had more or less echoed from the old Virginia bill of rights. (This is rather odd since he who had been the principal defender of the Declaration of Independence only two years before, now appeared to think that people never were created "equal.")[11] The Constitution also recommended public support for both religion and learning as Adams had wished, and was a good adaptation of those ideas of checks and balances he had always recommended. As he complacently and learnedly said, it was also "Locke, Sidney, and Rousseau and DeMably reduced to practice." He never was one to lack authorities.

It was also to be a thing of "laws and not of men," as the instrument reads, although lawyer Adams was primarily concerned with the independence of the judiciary as against the legislative and executive branches of government and these may not have been his own words. He must have resolved that the new frame of government be similar to what the people of Massachusetts had known under their old Charter, as well as similar, of course, to what he had advised all states to follow in his *Thoughts on Government* in 1776. It is interesting that his old friend in Congress, Richard Henry Lee of Virginia who disliked the "aristocratic genius" of the South, was especially anxious that the best kind of a government should be founded in Massachusetts where Lee said he hoped to end his days.[12]

Adams's visit to America in 1779 must have seemed later almost like a brief interval. Within a few months he was to return abroad, even before the work of the Constitutional Convention had been completed. He again took his servant and eleven-year-old John Quincy Adams—but now against the boy's wishes although he was accompanied by nine-year-old Brother Charles. It is strange that

Adams while in America had never visited the Congress to report on his first trip to France, instead had resorted to letters. Perhaps this was because Adams detested its "dirty politics," perhaps because the Congress had changed in composition although he still had some good friends there. Whatever the reason, he had kept his distance but had promptly accepted the new Congressional appointment to be Minister Plenipotentiary to make peace and commercial agreements with Great Britain. His promptness in accepting the new commission, which vindicated his record in France, may seem amazing. It is amazing, however, only if one forgets the agony through which Congress had been going in recent months, partly because of the Deane affair and partly because of its own fearful attitude about foreign policy, which included territorial settlements in the West and the question of the New England fisheries. It is amazing only if one forgets all the political wrangling entailed, of which John Adams had surely been aware.[13]

Again taking the perilous winter voyage, in the leaky old *Sensible*, the Adams group landed in December, 1779, at Port Ferrol, Spain. Then, after attending the theater in Madrid, they endured a long and difficult overland trip to France by mules, horses, and rotten old carriages, reaching Paris in February, 1780.

Adams's frosty reception by Vergennes was soon succeeded by the complete eruption of all good relations. The French had suspected but not known about the commercial agreements which the Americans were now proposing to make with England in case of "peace" (in addition, of course, to a recognition of American independence). The French were concerned lest the "Peace Party" should take over the American Congress. Concerned with his ally, Spain (not an ally of the United States), and Spain's interest in securing Gibraltar from the English, Vergennes resented the "shirt-sleeve" diplomacy which the blunt Adams now advanced.[14]

France and America seemed hopelessly divided. Adams even thought that America had been too free in expressing her gratitude to France. Since Vergennes was subsequently joined by Franklin in resenting Adams's attitude, and since the latter now considered himself of no use in Paris, he took himself and his boys in July to Holland where antiEnglish sentiment was soon to result in war. There, in lieu of Henry Laurens, a former President of Congress soon languishing in the Tower of London, he settled down to cultivating the Dutch "Patriot" party, and tried to make a loan. He associated with literary and political men and propagandized above all with publishers, trying to teach the true cause of the struggling Americans. The "Patriot" party in Holland was unfortunately opposed by the proEnglish party of the Stadtholder of the House of Orange. The Adams boys, put in a Latin school in Amsterdam were soon transferred to Leyden, on complaint of the Master about John Quincy's attitude.[15]

Although the *Autobiography* breaks off early in 1780 when Adams was still in France, and the diary is silent for 1781 and early 1782, quite a bit is known about this period of Adams's career. There is the recently edited *Family Correspondence,* in addition to what Charles Francis Adams published in the "Official Correspondence"; as well as Adams's later protests to Mrs. Warren, and of course his later comments in 1809-1812 in the Boston *Patriot* (unfortunately written in white heat haste). The charge of old Dr. Franklin, although belonging to another period, may almost be said to belong to this: that while Adams meant well for his country and was always an honest man and often a wise one, he was sometimes absolutely out of his senses.[16]

If Franklin had been right in rejecting Adams's role in Paris in 1780, Adams was eventually to prove himself correct in making his audacious appeal to the Dutch, even if it took time.[17] The "stagnant" Dutch waters were once to make him seriously ill (presumably with some form of malaria, since his recovery was to be assisted with the "bark," i.e., quinine, cinchona or "Jesuits' Bark") and his self-reliance in this period cannot be too greatly emphasized. He was to meet with disappointment in the Lowlands for many, many months. Despite his fondness for the Dutch he was not even recognized as Minister Plenipotentiary until early 1782 and did not get a treaty until later. The commerce of the Dutch may have been in a state of decline, and they may have long resented the attitude of the English and shown a keen interest in the new American trade, but even war with England could not persuade them to recognize American independence at first. An armed neutrality of the North was meantime promising to emerge under the leadership of Catherine of Russia. Despite slow going at first, the courage of Adams eventually paid high dividends.

The diplomatic complications of the new "minister" to Holland, who soon replaced Laurens formally, were the complications of the entire European system which he had once hoped to avoid. In addition to France's favoring the Spanish claims (and, according to Congress, France was always to be consulted in making any peace with England), there were the endless fears and hopes of many

Continental powers, several being exposed to "shirt-sleeve," or "militia," diplomacy by still another of the Lees.

The appointment of Robert R. Livingston in 1781 to handle foreign matters for the Congress introduced a new professional note in the conduct of American affairs, but this was another thorn in Adams's side. Livingston, plainly under the influence of the "French Party" at home was critical of some of Adams's actions in Holland.[18]

Despite such French influence, Adams still retained friends of foreign affairs in the Congress who supported his work abroad, notably James Lovell of Massachusetts who had made a few epistolary passes at Abigail while John was in Europe—until she put him in his place in 1781.[19] There were other family problems. Young John Quincy Adams had accompanied Francis Dana as a clerk in the latter's futile role of minister to Russia in 1781, thus rendering the father more lonely than ever, for his son Charles had returned to America, homesick.

So John Adams remained more or less alone in Holland, returning only briefly to Paris in the summer of 1781 to rebuff efforts by Russia and Austria at "mediation." He experienced several attacks of the fever, as did also his servant, but recovered his health by horseback riding. There was little but courage and a sense of self-importance to sustain him.

In spite of Adams's insistence that independence for the "United States" always come first in any negotiation (he hated the expression, "colonies"), and while opposing all French and Spanish intrigue, he still retained something of his old ambivalence or sense of values. While scornfully turning down the idea of a European "Congress" to mediate in 1781, he favored the idea a year later since this action seemed to mean that the independence of his country would be universally recognized. While defying Livingston's proFrench instructions in 1781, not to force his credentials on the States-General in Holland, he later acknowledged that gentleman's authority to some extent.[20]

The year 1782 was much better. Dutch recognition of Adams's official role as Minister Plenipotentiary having finally been secured, the Hotel des Etats-Unis was purchased at The Hague as an American legation.[21] A Dutch loan was also completed. Adams's persistence, one might almost say his patience, had finally paid off. Although some of his friends in America seemed to think that he had leisure for writing, were they ever to exchange places with him, as he once wrote Abigail, they would see for themselves "what a pretty Thing it is to be an American Minister."[22] He was busier than ever.

The really significant thing in 1782 was the change in the British government. The North administration had fallen in March, and the Whig, Shelburne ("The Jesuit of Berkeley Square"), had succeeded the dead Rockingham as Prime Minister, in July. The opposition was now in power and because of the international situation the English decision to accept peace with the Americans, even independence if necessary, was now a basis for negotiation. Adams felt that his publications had influenced Shelburne.[23]

But what about our ally, France, and her ally, Spain, which coveted Gibraltar and had been assured that the French would seek that end? What about Congressional instructions to heed the former? What about the Loyalists? What about the Mississippi question and Spain, the New England fisheries, and other territorial problems in the New World?

The American commissioners for peace with England were now five in number, Jefferson and Laurens having been added to the ranks of Jay, Franklin, and Adams. There seemed to have been doubt in some quarters in America about Adams in 1781, and the Congress had acted against him on motion of the Virginian, James Madison, who distrusted Adams's impulsiveness, his New Englandism, and his antiFrench stand. However, Laurens had retired to the south of France, and Jefferson had not yet come over to Europe, so that only old, gouty Dr. Franklin, the dignified Jay (disgusted with all Bourbons as a result of his long residence in Madrid), and John Adams, remained to make the peace.

Adams immediately expressed feelings—to himself, at least—that Dr. Franklin had kept him in the dark about the earliest negotiations.[24] He also feared that Franklin might try to influence John Jay, who had recently arrived in Paris from Madrid. He was soon glad to find that Jay would side with himself. Indeed, he even wondered if Jay might not be too antiFrench. The upright and embittered Jay, with his Huguenot background, despised all Bourbons to the point where he would be willing to ignore his instructions, if necessary to preserve American honor,[25] and Adams agreed. Congress simply did not know what was going on, they thought.

The most serious charge against the American peace commissioners is that in making peace in 1782 they did in spirit evade their instructions, i.e., to keep France informed about everything and not to make peace without her. This was eventually done in a formal sense, but a nice question arises about the means employed. Even Franklin had gone along with his colleagues. Their fears were apparently groundless. When Franklin finally informed Vergennes of the preliminary (really definitive) agreements of 1782, he found the French Foreign Minister glad to know that the Americans had gotten such generous terms.[26]

Vergennes did, however, express anger later in complaining that the shrewd American commissioners had lacked "courtesy" in the proceedings. It was a charge of ill-breeding and ingratitude for which Franklin immediately apologized, as he pressed his request for still more financial aid from France. Perhaps Vergennes was merely expressing the complaint of any traditional diplomat who resented "shirt-sleeve" methods. Or perhaps he did not like some of the "ugly Americans."

As Adams had feared, England had at least partially succeeded in the "preliminary" negotiations in separating America from France. The terms had been generous. American independence had been recognized, the New England fisheries secured, the land to the Mississippi and Northwards saved (a separate article about the boundaries of West Florida unfortunately was "secret" diplomacy), and only the Loyalists had received weak treatment. About the latter, old Dr. Franklin had been especially vehement, perhaps because a once beloved son of his had become one of the best known of Loyalists, and Franklin's reputation was at stake. He eventually denied that "Tories" should receive consideration at all, as the English had vainly hoped.[27]

Of course, Congress was indignant at the cavalier treatment accorded the ally, France, and Foreign Secretary Livingston proceeded to criticize the commissioners severely; but Adams rejoiced. "It is a glory to have broken such infamous orders," he wrote.[28] He alternated attacks on the character of Franklin in 1782 with violent attacks on the French court. He even saw himself as the protector of the Dutch, with whom he would make alliance against the French if necessary; and he visited London in October, 1783.

The preliminary peace negotiations with England had revealed Adams a remarkable man. He had once again shown himself ambivalent in character. He could be antiFrench and proFrench in the same breath; could hate the English even while favoring their commerce to America; and could oppose all "Tories" even while expressing compassion for *emigrés* in England. He had shown himself to be as flexible and opportunistic as anyone could have been under the circumstances. As he once wrote of the situation, one should never stand on ceremony when escaping danger. His "suspicions" had paid off.

Fortunately, Abigail and daughter Nabby came over to Europe in 1784, reuniting with John Adams after five long years, and seeing John Quincy Adams, the eldest son, now returned from St. Petersburg. The family settled for a year at Auteuil, France, only a few miles from the heart of Paris, in a scrumptious estate with lovely gardens that John Adams had rented from the Comte de Rouhault. It was near the Bois de Boulogne where Adams took a daily walk, primarily for reasons of health but also because he enjoyed it.[29] The residence of the Adamses at Auteuil is a charming idyll, but the family did not go out in public much. Abigail did attend the French opera but little else. Etiquette did not require their being presented at court.

Nineteen-year-old Nabby (named Abigail after her mother, and commonly referred to as Abigail the second), is said to have been a shy and pretty girl who had been having an affair with a certain Royall Tyler in Braintree, and was being given a chance in 1784 to reconsider the whole affair. She had been whisked off to Europe by her parents largely for this purpose. The adage that "absence makes the heart grow fonder" apparently did not apply in her case. Indeed, John Adams, at a distance, had at the beginning disapproved of Tyler, a popular young lawyer of good family but in Adams's opinion a "popinjay" (although later a most successful dramatist, and subsequently Chief Justice of Vermont). The father had once wished the whole affair off, although he had said that of course this would have to depend on Nabby's own judgment, aided by that of her mother and her relatives, i.e., her aunts and uncles, their brothers and sisters, etc., etc.. The poor girl never had a chance. She was to marry two years later, in London in 1786 a Colonel William Smith, an American Chargé des Affaires under her father. Young Smith was dashing and brave, but unfortunately had grandiose and speculative ideas. Nabby did give him a number of children, however, the first born in London; but he was to become a constant worry to the Adamses.

It is interesting that Royall Tyler had once owned the old Vassall-Borland summer house in Braintree, which the Adamses later bought. It had been confiscated during the Revolution from the "genteel" and Episcopal Vassalls as a Loyalist estate, and sold by a brother-in-law of Abigail, who was acting as an agent for Massachusetts and who wanted to buy the place himself. It had been returned to the Vassall heirs after the war and then purchased by Tyler. Here was the house (without eighty-three acres) the Adamses secured as a new residence when they should return from England. The estate, what their descendants were later to call "the Old House," is today known in Quincy as the Adams National Historic Site. It is the same place (minus the farm lands and considerably refurbished, of course) to which Tyler had once hoped to take his bride, and his rejection by Nabby would seem to have made the place something of an embarrassment to the Adamses, but it never did.[30]

All through the months in France John Adams had desperately hoped for an appointment to England. Despite his earlier hatred for that country he apparently still regarded England with affection, perhaps another instance of his ability to be ambivalent. The appointment, which sent him and his family first to a London hotel in 1785 and then to the legation in Grosvenor Square, was a deeply cherished one. It is a pity that his stay did not turn out better.

The Adamses found English society polite but cold and unresponsive. Why John Adams should have expected anything else, except for his incurable optimism, is a mystery. Even when he was introduced to George III he merely found him courteous. Abigail was later to say that the Queen was no friend to her, but since she preferred her "hens and chickings" to the characters at Court, she, too, could scarcely have expected otherwise.[31]

So the English venture was officially a disappointment. Even trade with the British West Indies was forbidden to American ships, and Lord Sheffield's argument in favor of Great Britain's resuming her old navigational exclusiveness remained official policy. For some strange reason John Adams had thought that the British would join in his policy of free trade everywhere, even after the American Revolution. He never did succeed in getting a treaty of commerce.

Adams did go back twice to Holland, once to borrow more money for the youthful republic. The Adamses also got out into the provinces—John disliked the smoke and damp of London—visiting that curious bachelor, Thomas Brand-Hollis, and of course Stratford-on-Avon; but whether they enjoyed England better than France remains doubtful, even though they had lived longer in the former and of course their daughter had married in London.[32]

What John Adams did in his private capacity in England is another thing. His attitude towards the American Loyalists is especially interesting. Since all meetings with Loyalists were painful, he avoided them as much as possible. Perhaps the Loyalists as a whole did not like him. One exception was made with his "dear old friend,"

Jonathan Sewall (and his wife, the former Esther Quincy of Braintree), who afterwards said that Adams was warm in his attachments but rather implacable towards those he thought his enemies.[33]

In early 1787 Adams published the first volume of his three volume *Defence of the Constitutions of Government of the United States of America,* written in idleness and anger. The *Defence* ostensibly dealt with the earliest American state constitutions and the principles that lay behind them; but it is really a collection of learned thought by philosophers of all ages about principles of government and about all kinds of government. Adams commented freely, especially in Volume One. As one reviewer correctly put it (presumably that "wretch," Silas Deane), the work actually says little about the subject.[34]

It should be remembered that Adams had chiefly engineered the Massachusetts Constitution of 1780 but only after M. Turgot had made his criticism, and must have had its principles in mind when he wrote the *Defence.* However, he had always cherished a balance of powers, and had so advised all the states as early as 1776.

The *Defence* has been called a lawyer's brief, and in piling evidence upon evidence, is, in fact, so. Although all three volumes act primarily as a defense against the criticism of Turgot (one of whose complaints was that the American states were too imitative of England, which made Adams "exult"), it is in the first volume that Adams launched his attack upon the idea of natural equality and upon the idea that a single chambered legislature can ever make democracy work. The "democratical branch" is always in danger, he said. A "simple" democracy can never work.

Checks and balances between the executive and legislative branches are required, he thought, for one thing because there is always bound to be an aristocracy, even in a republic. A natural aristocracy—"The rich, the well-born and the able"—is inevitable, he argued, and provision for this should be made in a second legislative chamber, or senate. (Whether Adams meant by this that he really believed in an aristocracy, as later charged, is a most important point, reflecting as it does on his own undoubted aspirations.)

A strong first magistrate, or executive, is another necessity, according to the *Defence.* There always has to be some kind of "subordination," Adams argued, that of offices if of nothing else. Parties are of course a danger and should be controlled, he thought, but he gave them scant attention.

Adams had always taught that the people are sovereign and that the happiness of the greatest number always be sought, but he bluntly stated in the *Defence* that all men are governed by their interests or passions. He obviously believed in a "free society" in a government of "laws and not of men," but did not answer the embarrassing question which Turgot had raised, "What if a law is unjust?"

Adams's ideas in the *Defence* were no doubt the result of his book learning, but his ideas must also have grown out of his experience in Continental Europe and in England, and above all because of the news from America about the Shays Rebellion. That resistance to public authority was breaking out in his own beloved Massachusetts, for whose Constitution he had been the "principal engineer," was most alarming, and he hurried-up work on the *Defence*. As he later explained, his countrymen seemed to be running wild, being exposed to too much *Common Sense* and such popular works, all of which he said were weak on the true "construction" of a free government.[35]

Needless to say, the *Defence,* or what was to be taken out of context, was later to embarrass John Adams in American political life. Abigail had warned him that in America he would be considered as wanting to set up a king. The work had been hurriedly written, and he almost immediately called it pedantic and later even "dull," but its principles were to remain life-long convictions. The structure of government, which he considered a "science," had always been a part of his concern. Parties and politics were subordinate evils which he had always despised.

John and Abigail left England in the summer of 1788 to return to America seemingly without any pangs or tears, although their experience in England must have left its mark.[36] They were greeted in Boston with enthusiasm. If republics are notoriously ungrateful, John Adams did not know this, at first. The recently purchased one time Loyalist estate, the Borland-Vassall house in Braintree (no small farmhouse for them, now) was quite satisfactory, except that the rooms were small and the ceilings low. Abigail called it a "wren's nest."[37] She used the family coach with its coat-of-arms without any open comment by the neighbors and was using the Quincy coat-of-arms years later when John reproved her because of the publicity that might result. The statesman-scholar had finally come home after ten years abroad, bringing many lovely things, especially from France and Holland, with which to decorate the new home. Whether the ideas he had brought were to ornament his country is more debatable.

He was going to retire on his laurels and be a farmer, and Abigail a dairymaid.

CHAPTER 7

A Friend of Federalism

"I am as much a republican as I was in 1775"

JOHN Adams was only fifty-three when he returned to Braintree in 1788, and Abigail about forty-four, yet he gloomily considered himself an old man whose life's work had been accomplished, and he fussed about finances.[1] If he had known that he was to live another forty years and hold high office in his country, he might not have been so sure. He once suggested to his eldest son, John Quincy, that they go into law together; and he must have considered this a possibility although nothing came of it. Actually, John Quincy, who had been at Harvard and was studying law in the office of Theophilus Parsons of Newburyport (an originator of the Essex Junto and whose ideas had been supported by John Adams in the Massachusetts Convention in 1779), was to go it alone in the law until his appointment by Washington to The Hague in 1794.

The father may have worried about finances, but his energy, as always, seemed boundless. It now extended to all kinds of farm work. He and John Quincy even tossed manure together. Adams senior was in good health and said he was contented, although he missed the bookshops and the society of men-of-letters he had known in England. He had found his "estate" in disorder on his return, and it had required all his attention to repair it. There was a fine brook by the house where he now lived.[2]

As for public affairs in America, there was a great increase in population, and provisions were plenty and cheap; and agriculture, commerce, the fisheries, and manufactures were all better than he had expected; but there was a great shortage of money.

This scarcity of money must have affected John Adams like any other farmer, even if Abigail was as good a dairymaid as one could wish for. Economics were always considered in the Adams family.

69

Public office had not appealed to John Adams, at first. He refused to join the old Congress which he had once called nothing but a diplomatic assemblage of the states and then refused to be considered as a Federal Senator from Massachusetts because the office would be beneath him. He plainly favored a higher office. This suited Alexander Hamilton who was "arranging" the first elections, that Adams would be content with "second" place, i.e., not to oppose Washington.[3] There is no reason to think that Hamilton was in any way anti-Adams at this time, though Adams did resent Hamilton's scattering of the electoral vote when he later learned about it.

People in general, at least people in New England, seem to have thought that high office for John Adams was only his due, thus agreeing with him. He was more popular than he had feared the *Defence* would make him, the times favoring his ideas about lawlessness and what was considered political chaos. Moreover, he had come to favor the new "Federal" Constitution, although he was shortly to conclude that its sovereignty could not be divided. He considered it a national government, in fact, and constructed somewhat along lines that he had always advocated. It even had a bicameral legislature although the Senate had too much power, he thought, and an executive that he hoped would be independent enough especially in foreign affairs.[4]

In 1788 and later John Adams exemplified the farmer in politics, long a prime plank in Federalism in an America that was still overwhelmingly agricultural, as he thought it would be for a long, long time.

Yet there was something curiously different about John Adams. He still kept up his acquaintance with Dr. Priestly, the Deist whom all Federalists were supposed to detest. He once said that he had not changed his principles, and that "I . . . am as much a republican as I was in 1775"; but his own son, John Quincy, had not only been antiFederal in 1778 but had been surprised to learn that his father favored the new Constitution. "Republican" principles somehow seemed to be at stake, according to the son, who must have thought that he knew his father well. Apparently he had been mistaken, not knowing how ambivalent his father could be.[5]

The electoral vote of 1789 is an interesting one. Although Hamilton had scattered the "second" vote, as already noted, some other people must have agreed. There were several "second" votes for Hancock whom Adams disliked (although he did not hate him as he later did Hamilton whom he once compared to a worm), but the interesting thing is the almost universal vote against Adams on the part of the Southern states. He must have been considered something of a "Yankee." It should be remembered that each elector in the College had two votes, and "scattering" refers to the "second" vote. Some people naturally feared the antiFederalists, especially George Clinton of New York.[6]

Adams thought the outcome a "scurvey" affair. "Is this Justice?" he demanded, "Is there common sense or decency in this business?"[7]

He had got only thirty-four votes in the Electoral College as against Washington's (unanimous) sixty-nine, but since this was the second highest, it made Adams the Vice President. Although it was, he said, only love of his country which made him accept the office at all, he actually beat Washington in journeying to New York City, the temporary seat of the new government, in April, 1789. Abigail followed later.

There was something ironical in Vice President John Adams presiding over the Senate of the United States, a body he thought necessary to house aristocrats. "His Rotundity" was no aristocrat, himself, although he was to protest that the Boylston family of his mother had always been rich and famous and that he himself was not of "obscure" origin.[8] The Senate was to prove itself anything but aristocratic, however, having some plain "republican" members who, when defeated, had friends in the lower House to sustain them. In short, the Senate from the first proved itself more political than social. One of its earliest conflicts arose over whether the proper way to address President Washington was perhaps as "His Most Highness"—and how to treat him, generally. The opposition won, especially in the House of Representatives, and plain titles succeeded, through default.

The charge of holding "titles" never was to vanish entirely, however, and what Adams had stated in the *Defence* now began to be used against him. He was even accused of holding "monarchical" views and of favoring an inheritable Presidency. His letters to Roger Sherman and to Samuel Adams, on the limitations of "popular" sovereignty, seemed to support such ideas. He had been too much impressed abroad, they thought, especially with the English "mixed" form of government. His "Discourses on Davila," articles in the news press in 1790, appeared to be more of the same. These latter (really a continuation of the *Defence)*, Adams's comments about what an Italian had written about France during the religious wars of the seventeenth century, even Alexander Hamilton criticized because the articles could weaken confidence in the new Federal government.[9]

The French Revolution had had its share in arousing such risibilities, for Adams had opposed it almost from the beginning, denying that it was at all like the American Revolution and lamenting the omnipotent pretensions of the French National Assembly.[10] He echoed Edmund Burke in England, an old friend of the Americans who seemed to have turned apostate. (Perhaps Adams should be called "The American Burke.") A quarrel with Jefferson even reached upwards into the Cabinet in 1791, for Jefferson had "endorsed" an American edition of Tom Paine's *The Rights of Man* (dedicated to President Washington), deploring the "heresies" which he said had recently appeared in America. He later denied to Adams that he ever had had him (Adams) in mind, but his "disingenuous" last letter to Adams was never answered. The two men were to be enemies henceforth, for many, many years, even if the formal record sometimes looks otherwise.

Meantime, the "Publicola" letters, which had occasioned the quarrel, had been appearing in the press, defending Adams and attacking Jefferson, although not by name. They were naturally attributed to the elder Adams but had in fact been written by his eldest son, John Quincy, who once again proved his filial obedience.[11]

This quarrel between Jefferson and Adams ("The Duke of Braintree") in 1791 parallels in point of time the quarrel between Jefferson and Hamilton over the constitutionality of the Bank of the United States, but it had started earlier because of the "Discourses on Davila." That, in turn, had been paralleled by the old quarrel over the assumption of states' debts, a prime Hamiltonian measure which had helped to turn James Madison against the administration.

Adams conducted himself as Vice President with his usual willingness to do duty, even if he did consider it an "insignificant" office. He was also methodical in personal life, eating a heavy breakfast, reading the newspapers, smoking cigars, and taking a daily walk. Abigail continued to be a cheery helpmate believing as always that a "cheerful heart" is the best antidote for evil. The Adamses were now living in Bush Hill, Philadelphia (where Abigail was having trouble in finding a good cook), the capital having been temporarily located for a second time. They had moved from their enjoyable New York home on Richmond Hill. Regretably, Abigail was often ill, and for this as well as for reasons of economy the family continued to use Braintree (or Quincy, as the North Precinct soon was called) as a place of refuge. Washington had similarly used Mount Vernon as a place for peace and comfort.

The five thousand dollar salary which Adams received as Vice President was not as much as he and Abigail really needed, but even so they were able to get by, and perhaps even to save a little. Other persons in high office found themselves running steadily behind, this being especially true of the Secretary of State, Thomas Jefferson, who, like most Virginians, lived in a lavish way. Adams wondered why Jefferson did not live as frugally as himself.

Despite his blundering "Discourses on Davila," Adams received seventy votes in the Electoral College of 1792 (Washington was again elected unanimously with one hundred and thirty-two votes), which again made Adams Vice President. Ominously, however, the anti-Federalists had supported George Clinton with fifty votes.[12] Adams saw behind all this the spirit of Jefferson, whose soul, he thought, was taken up with the "blind spirit of party." The antiFederalists expected to make even greater inroads in the Congressional elections to follow.[13]

The second administration of Washington was marked by the unfortunate Genêt affair, the problem of neutrality, the resignation of Jefferson, and by all kinds of political uproar. Even Boston and Cousin Sam Adams were infected with a proFrench spirit. "The Anti-Federal party," Vice President Adams wrote his son in 1793, "by their ox feasts and their civic feasts, their King-killing toasts, their perpetual insolence and billingsgate against all the nations and governments of Europe, their everlasting brutal cry of tyranny, despots, and combinations against liberty, etc., etc., etc., have probably irritated, offended, and provoked all the crowned heads of Europe at last; and a little more of this indelicacy and indecency may involve us in a war with all the world."[14]

The collapse in early 1792 in a rage of speculation, in government securities as well as in land, had added to a general concern. Such concern was also true for Adams. There was too much easy money being made. He even came to believe that banks, except those of simple deposit, were fraudulent.[15] His was a countryman's view. He had supported Hamilton's financial schemes earlier but had now broken with him and them, no longer thinking of himself as a "lightning rod" for "federal" experiments. The economic collapse in 1792, foreshadowing the more terrible collapse in 1797, which was to ruin Robert Morris as well as Charles Adams and to injure Adams's son-in-law, was about what he had expected.

In his second term, President Washington had become the chief target of abuse; Vice President Adams was no longer the prime enemy in the eyes of the opposition. The "Duke of Braintree" had abandoned his wig and ceremonial sword.[16] President Washington was repeatedly attacked in the press, especially by the Philadelphia *Aurora,* edited by a grandson of Benjamin Franklin (whom Adams had known as a boy in France) whose family is said to have resented Washington's cool treatment of the "Venerable Sage." These attacks were attributed to Washington's declaration of neutrality in April 1793, and because of the treaty with England which Chief Justice John Jay made the following year.[17] The background for the issues had been American concern for neutral rights in which both France and England had been offenders. Still, France was an "ally," and there was much enthusiasm for the idea of revolution which France had once helped in America and which seemed to be continuing abroad. There was even some talk of war with England. Other foreign problems, such as that of the Algerian pirates, paled by comparison.

Vice President Adams gave support to the idea of neutrality and then for Jay's Treaty.[18] He echoed what his eldest son had said in the papers during and after the Genêt affair: that self-preservation is the first law of nature ("nature" was a great argument for anything in the eighteenth century), and that the restoration of France to her West Indies possessions, which the United States had guaranteed, would open their inhabitants to all the bloodshed that seemed to accompany the French Revolution everywhere.[19] There was also the Hamiltonian contention that the old Alliance had been made with the King of France and not with the people of France, and therefore was inoperative. Jefferson, the Secretary of State, denied this,[20] and probably was right.

Although Adams had continued to detest the French Revolution, he had remained strangely detached in 1793 at the time that Jay's instructions were being approved by the Senate. His respect for foreign powers, perhaps a throwback to his years of diplomacy, shows him to have been speaking a different language from some of his fellow countrymen. He had done so in other ways from the days of the *Defence,* at least.

When the news came about the details of the treaty which Jay had made in England, though Adams thought it had at least prevented war, it did put him into something of a dilemma by arousing his old suspicions about European policies. It was not that he was pro-

British, in spite of his intense dislike for Revolutionary France; it was simply that there was a dilemma that would not be solved, or not at least until his own Presidential days.

Adams's support for Jay's treaty can be seen as a belated example of his former support for all "federal" ideas, as well as support for Washington's policy and for the benefit of his country. The old precept, "Rule or ruin," must often have seemed the only one to follow.

Of course, John Jay was a possible political competitor of Adams. The unpopularity of his treaty did not enhance his chances in 1796, as Adams noted.[21]

It had been suspected for some time that Washington would not seek a third term, but this prospect did not become a reality until the "Farewell Address" came out in September, 1796. Adams was then in a stronger position to be a successor than he was later.

The "campaign" of 1796 was really no campaign at all. It soon became evident that Jefferson would be the chief rival to Adams, but both "candidates" eschewed politics, both hating it. Neither actively sought the office, although Adams needed and probably desired it.[22] "The Heir Apparent," as Adams often sarcastically referred to himself, said that he would not serve as Vice President under Jefferson; but the latter had commissioned Madison, in an open letter, to instruct the House of Representatives, in case there should be a tie, that preference be given Adams who had always been his "senior."[23]

Adherents of both men, or adherents of their "parties," nevertheless turned what was basically a sectional struggle into one of the most abusive in American history. Everything possible was raked up about both men. The Federalists, however, were considerably divided, many Southerners (as well as Hamilton, originally) pushing Thomas Pinckney of South Carolina. Pinckney was not so well known but he had been recently the author of a favorable treaty with Spain which had ricocheted from the unpopular treaty Jay had made in London. Adams finally won by a narrow margin, largely because of New England support as well as that of his "party," and because he had a supporter in Virginia and in several other places. Still, he became President by only three votes (seventy-one to sixty-eight), something the opposition would never let him forget, and something that he himself could never forget. He became President by "accident," though the phrase probably conceals his real popular strength.[24]

Even one of the opposition, the outspoken William B. Giles of Virginia, said that "the old man" would make a good President, only that it would sometimes be necessary to "check" him a little. Perhaps that is what many of the so-called opposition always thought.

"The old man" had spent the summer of 1796 in erecting a new barn on his land in Quincy.[26] Even if he sometimes thought of himself as the "heir apparent" in politics, he also still thought of himself primarily as a farmer, and of Abigail as a farmer's wife.

CHAPTER 8

Mr. President

"You ought to give me credit for it"

THE Adams administration has been identified with the collapse of Federalism, but internal weakness had already appeared. Adams had been selected in the Electoral College in 1796 without the confidence of the Federalist leaders.[1] He was President "by accident" of the voters. Sectionalism had also played a large role in voting in the College. Adams may have been a farmer but he was also a New England man. Just as Burr had been ignored by Southerners in 1796 in order to protect Jefferson, so Pinckney had been ignored by Northerners in order to protect Adams. It is interesting that Adams recommended Burr as a Brigadier General in 1798. Both men considered themselves to have been badly treated two years before.[2]

Although Washington had viewed with increasing alarm the tendency towards political divisions, parties were not yet fully formed. Federalists (or "Moneycrats" or "Monarchists," as they were variously called) and antiFederalists (or "Republicans," in "honor" of the French Republic) were not yet strictly party men. Sectionalism was still strong as Washington had warned in his "Farewell Address." Unfortunately, the Adams administration, apparently born to trouble, was to see further party development take place, especially after 1798. Jefferson, himself, although not antiAdams and not a candidate for the presidency in 1796 was to consider himself something of a "party" leader in later years.[3]

Adams was soon to ignore Vice President Jefferson as an executive colleague, just as Washington had ignored Adams as an executive Vice President after 1791. Jefferson soon thought of himself primarily as a legislative figure.[4] Politics had something to do with this attitude. The principal thing that Adams and Jefferson had in

77

common in these years was their common dislike for Hamilton, Jefferson partly by nature, the former because of the "Pinckney Plot" in 1796. Abigail eventually was to label Hamilton as "Machiavellian."

Adams seems to have viewed himself as a President whose policies were continuous with Washington's, and he actually kept on most of the Cabinet. He always walked in the shadow of the former President. He thought of himself as being like Washington, a leader of all the people.[5] His independent view of the chief executive office also naturally angered many, especially Republicans. He was considered "antiFrench." Even President Washington had been suspect for this by some Republicans, in recent years, and some had even proposed Washington's impeachment in the last year of his second term.[6]

The opposition to President Adams was renewed by Republicans not just because he kept the Washington Cabinet more or less intact, but because it included several confidential friends of Hamilton. Adams apparently thought that he was continuing a "national" Cabinet. To give him his due, however, he did not for years suspect "treachery" on the part of Hamilton's friends, nor was he ever to believe this true of Wolcott of Connecticut.[7]

It nevertheless seems strange that Adams should have continued with these friends of Hamilton, i.e., Timothy Pickering, the Secretary of State, James McHenry, the Secretary of War, and Oliver Wolcott, the Secretary of the Treasury. President Washington in his second term had apparently been under Hamilton's influence, and the latter's friends in the Cabinet of the Adams's administration merely continued the practice they had already begun. Adams must often have seemed a weak man to them because of his acquiescence and uncharacteristic mildness.

Republicans had at first seemed favorable to President Adams to the dismay of all dyed-in-the-wool Federalists.[8] The latter disliked Adams's fondness for the French people even though they recognized his dislike of French revolutionary governments and his admiration for the English government while disliking English upper society. Extreme Federalists never did approve Adams having a foot in each camp. They never understood his ambivalent nature. They later considered him a turncoat because of his dislike of "party spirit."

Republican favor for the Adams administration was soon to vanish, however, as the new President became more antiFrench. The old problem of neutrality again raised its head. The French Directory went so far as to describe all American seamen found in British vessels as nothing but "pirates."

International discord had been intensified when Washington had recalled the American envoy to France, James Monroe, in 1796. Adams had inherited this situation. The original charge against Monroe was that he had been too apologetic about the Jay Treaty, but Adams later called him "stupid." (Monroe's embarassing behavior was to be repeated under President Jefferson in 1806, so he cannot have been an ideal diplomat at any time.[9]) Jefferson's refusal to take Monroe's place in France—he considered Adams's behavior after making the offer as rather cool—and then Madison's refusal, was to prolong the *impasse*.[10] C. C. Pinckney of South Carolina was chosen to be Monroe's replacement but the French Directory refused to receive him.

The French Directory continued in its arrogant way, refusing in 1798 to recognize the new commissioners without "bribery," i.e., in the XYZ affair, the initials by which Adams called the French agents. The Directory always had exaggerated ideas about "Republican" strength in America. M. de Talleyrand, the leading French minister, originally a party to the attempt at "bribery," eventually recognized the extravagance of such ideas, and showed a more pacifistic attitude in 1799 when Adams decided to reopen negotiations.[11]

President Adams was at first concerned about the number of Federalists who were dropping out of national political life. Extreme Federalism was, apparently, rapidly turning into "Hamiltonianism." It was revived as a general idea in 1798 when the idea of war against France was popular; but this in turn raised the cry of "militarism" which Adams disliked, although he was always in favor of strengthening the navy.[12] The decline in warlike spirit the following year (and perhaps the rebuff which Adams's son-in-law, Smith, had received in the Senate), was subsequently to support him in independent action.

Even in this later development, however, Hamilton was to appear prominently, being Washington's choice for second place in the military force to be raised against France. Perhaps it was General Washington's death late in 1799 which finally solved all difficulties for Adams.

The principal history of the Adams administration in foreign affairs thus consisted of the old quarrel over neutrality with both England and France, i.e., that "Free ships make free goods." Even the Alien and Sedition Acts of 1798, drafted by Federalists and signed into law by Adams[13] (and doubtless with Abigail's hearty concurrence, she being so enraged that she favored gagging the press to prevent any further abuse of her husband),[14] were only a part of the resentment against the proFrench element, which the problem of neutrality and the old French Alliance continued to raise. Adams had even encouraged a warlike spirit in America by releasing the news of the XYZ affair, thus inflaming the Congress which "abolished" the old French Alliance in unilateral but highly illegal fashion. An "undeclared" war with France existed at sea.

Adams was never so popular with the Federalist leaders and never so popular with those who love the sound of war, as in 1798. Not until he "reversed" himself in February, 1799, with the nomination of William Vans Murray (our minister at The Hague) as a new envoy to France, and not until he asked McHenry to resign and fired Timothy Pickering in May, 1800, did he really come into his own as an independent President. These actions of his appear to have been thoroughly justified as well as politically expedient, but the Hamiltonian Federalists fell into a fury claiming that Adams had ruined the party. Apparently they were wrong, but one can understand their anger and dismay. Adams was no longer a friend to Federalism as they understood it. Hamilton called him "an old woman."[15]

This decision of Adams in 1799 to renew relations with France, seeking peace instead of war, was to be the greatest claim to fame for his administration, even though he had alienated many. As he later wrote Mercy Warren, when protesting against the "errors" in her *History of the American Revolution,* "I think you ought to give me credit for it, instead of charging me with pride."

Among the many difficulties confronting President Adams were the troubles of his family, which, he said, gave him more worry than anything else. Abigail was frequently ill, necessitating long stays at Quincy (where John loved to live, anyway), and was using the Quincy coat of arms on her carriage.[16] There were even more troublesome problems about several of the children, especially Nabby and Charles. The former, with a vainglorious husband had had several children by him ("There will be statesmen in plenty, if Mrs. Smith goes from year to year in this way," Aunt Eliza had once wittily written); but Nabby led a precarious life that worried her parents.

Charles was even more of a problem. He was a heavy drinker. Even after his marriage in 1795 to Sally Smith, a marriage which his parents had bitterly opposed, a younger sister of the dashing Colonel who had married Nabby, he had persisted in his ways. He had been a handsome youth but had had troubles with reckless companions all his life. His father gradually hardened his heart against him. The "Old Man's" philosophy was that the weak and unlucky go to the wall. Indeed, Adams senior had passed through New York City in 1800 without seeing Charles, then in a most deplorable state. The dirty work of visiting the dying son was left to Abigail, on her trip through the city.[17]

Charles had originally been a promising law student in the New York office of Alexander Hamilton, no less, and the father had written politely about him at the time. Charles apparently had always displayed a brillance but lacked steadiness. He sometimes wept when he remembered the sum he owed his older brother, John Quincy Adams, and had invested unfortunately. He must have seemed to resemble his unfortunate uncle William, the brother of Abigail, who had deserted his family in Lincoln, Massachusetts, was once tried on charges of counterfeiting, and who had always loved a drink— perhaps he was a "preacher's son" (the uncle had died an early death, also).[18]

The brightest spot for the parents was the behavior of the eldest son, John Quincy, who had even put aside a love affair in Newburyport in 1788 at their request. When his mother had opposed that affair (John and Abigail always opposed their children falling in love) she had written that her illness and lack of strength prevented her from saying more. After a career of newspaper writing criticizing Paine's *Rights of Man,* and supporting the idea of neutrality, John Quincy had been appointed by Washington to The Hague in 1794, and then transferred to Prussia by his President Father.[19] He was to resign his diplomatic connection when he learned of his father's defeat in the race for reelection in 1800.

The frequent and long absences of President Adams in Quincy had raised some criticism, even disturbing Washington. However, Abigail apparently had been seriously ill in 1798, and the yellow fever the next summer had led the government temporarily to remove to Trenton. It was back in Philadelphia in May, 1800, when Adams, after an unusually long residence in Quincy, took his final independent step in disposing of McHenry and Pickering, which was to appear so precipitate an action to the Hamiltonians.

In thus declaring political war on the extreme leaders of the Federalist Party, Adams was making an appeal to the moderate and secondary Federalists, and to the rank and file of people. Men like John Marshall of Virginia, appointed by Adams to replace Pickering as Secretary of State and then appointed Chief Justice, also favored the new policy of Adams's independence because they hoped it would appeal to some Republicans. Early in the summer of 1800 Adams himself had contemplated heading up something like a third party, although he had never been a "party chief."[20]

The election of 1800 is interesting. The final result, seventy-three votes in the Electoral College for Jefferson and seventy-three votes for Burr, leaving Adams with only sixty-five, suggests that sectionalism was not as strong as it had been in 1796 but it also suggests that Adams was defeated primarily by a split party. Although he was bitterly to reflect that America no longer had any Americans, and that "The Federalists have been no more American than the Antis," he had really fallen between two stools.[21]

It has been argued with plausibility that Adams was more popular with the people in 1800 than in 1796,[22] but this ignores the extent to which "parties" operated in the latter year. "Farmer Adams" undoubtedly appealed to many. Yet it was organizational politics in various places, including Burr's efforts in New York, that determined the outcome. Hamilton's letter *(Letter . . . concerning the Public Conduct and Character of John Adams)* criticizing Adams but recommending that he be reelected, is of course important; but like the action of Charles Pinckney in the South Carolina legislature defies analysis. Perhaps Adams had been hoist with his own petard: he had once remarked that all important events are carried by narrow margins. Since there really was party organization and discipline in 1800 he was deluding himself in thinking that he somehow stood above the idea.[23] So was Jefferson, who in his inaugural address was to say that we are all Republicans, we are all Federalists. It may have been true, but it was meaningless.

Actually, both Adams and Jefferson were adherents of party policy regardless of how both professed to abhor the "party spirit." Men will always be loyal to something. That the "Tory" Bolingbroke had once written a book, *The Idea of A Patriot King,* which both Adams and Jefferson knew, warning against the evils of factions or politics, is surely one of the ironies of the eighteenth century. The American Revolution had made political organizations inevitable.

That Adams did not stay for the inaugural of his successor can only be attributed to personal pique. Washington had attended Adams's inaugural in 1797 and had courteously taken place behind him when Adams had been sworn in as the new President.[24]

CHAPTER 9

Early Retirement

"I doubt whether faithful history ever was or ever can be written"

THE life of John Adams "in retirement" in Quincy, beginning in 1801 when he was sixty-five, is sometimes called a patriarchship, but if this suggests to anyone that he had begun to "mellow" nothing could be further from the truth.[1] Adams's salient characteristics merely sharpened as he grew older, as apparently is frequently true. In his early years of "retirement" he was often to explode in wrath and disgust, passing judgment on men and women and events in a highly personal manner that can only be called extraordinary.

These are the years when John Adams was to become an autobiographer on different occasions and in varying moods;[2] when he was to tangle with Mercy Warren as to the nature of the American Revolution;[3] when he was angrily to send letters to the Boston *Patriot* in defense of his relations with France;[4] and when he was unblushingly to write Benjamin Rush of his fears that certain persons—not himself—were in danger of becoming deified.

It was in this latter connection that he once told Rush, "I doubt whether faithful history ever was or ever can be written." This would have been a more fitting epitaph for his proposed tombstone on Penns Hill in Quincy than the fact that he had made peace with France in 1800, which he had once suggested.[5]

The immediate months for Adams after his failure to be reelected to the Presidency were devoted to recovery. He had taken his defeat hard, blaming Federalists in the main. Soon after his defeat in 1800 he had written, "We federalists are much in the situation of the party of Bolingbroke and Harley, after the treaty of Utrecht, completely and totally routed and defeated," and that "No party, that ever existed, knew itself so little, or so vainly overrated its own influence and popularity, as ours." His comment that "A group of foreign liars, encouraged by a few ambitious native gentlemen," had discomfited the education, the virtue, and the property of the country, was obviously a slap at "Republicans."[6]

Adams in retirement read the classics and took refuge in Stoic philosophy. He compared himself to Cicero, and, like old Cincinnatus, took up farm work again. He could not return to the bar so he exchanged "honor and virtue" for "manure," he sarcastically said. At various times he labeled his land "Stony Field," "Peace Field," and finally, in imitation of Monticello, as "Montizello," perhaps reflecting the various periods of his retirement. He once sarcastically called himself the "Monarch of Stony Field," the "Count of Gull Island," the "Earl of Mount Arrarat," the "Marquis of Candlewood Hill," and the "Baron of Rocky Run."[7] The "Duke of Braintree" was going to have "titles"—at last!

In his early days of retirement at Quincy, Adams frequently rode his horse on the beach, and walked four or five miles each day in sight of the Blue Hills where his old "enemy," Thomas Hutchinson, had once had a home. Times had changed. Hutchinson's old place in Milton had been confiscated during the war as Loyalist property, and had been purchased and lived in for a while by Adams's old friend, General Warren.

In 1802, the task of healing having been completed, Adams began an "Autobiography," only to be momentarily diverted by his acquisition of the Mount Wollaston land. When his correspondence with Rush started in 1805,[8] his trenchant pen had already opened a period of sharp personal criticism that was to last until 1813. He was strongly opposed to Jefferson's administration, of course, but his hatred for Alexander Hamilton in particular continued to grow.

Adams's critical view of Jefferson in 1801 was a very natural thing considering his exasperated feelings following the election. He had inherited the whole panoply of abuse which had marked that unhappy occasion. He considered any advocate of "democracy" an enemy to true "republicanism." He went beyond this, however, in denying on one occasion that he had ever had any intimacy with Jefferson beyond their official civilities, and saying that while he wished Jefferson no ill and bore him no envy, he shuddered at "the calamities which I fear his conduct is preparing for his country: from a mean thirst of popularity, an inordinate amibition, and a want of sincerity."[9] These words were written in confidence in 1803 (unfortunately divulged for political reasons twenty years later), and should be balanced with the civil letter which Adams wrote Jefferson in 1801, in response to a kind letter about the death of Charles, expressing the wish that Jefferson might have a "quiet and prosperous administration."[10]

Of course Adams writhed at the Republican repeal of the Judiciary Act he had recommended as necessary, and with which his name was closely connected ("The Midnight Judges"), the impeachment of Chase, and the fact that Jefferson had pardoned the unspeakable Tom Callender. He and Abigail also resented the President's removal in 1802 of John Quincy Adams from a minor Federal post in Boston, although Jefferson was blandly to protest that he had not known that this was John Adams's son.

It was what Adams considered the weak foreign policy of Jefferson that eventually turned him so vehemently against the administration—that and the closely related weakness of the American navy, which Adams had always supported. Jefferson's actions showed a dislike of ships and shipping, especially that of New England, Adams thought. The affair of the *Chesapeake* in 1807 rankled, and the Embargo was a "cowardly" thing. Adams did not doubt the good intentions of Jefferson and Madison (proverbially leading to Hell, of course), but considered that both lacked judgment and candor. He was sure that Jefferson was leaving his country infinitely worse than he had found it.[11] Not until the newly elected President, James Madison, had appointed John Quincy Adams as a special minister to Russia in 1809 did he begin to change. Of course, he had always disliked diehard Federalists, especially the "Essex Junto" with their "Tory" opposition to American policy. He apparently disliked anyone labeled an extremist in political life.

The threat of war had never appeared to the "Old Man" so disgraceful a thing as British control of American shipping, i.e., the old problem of neutrality now enlarged by the "Rule of '56." He would not have avoided war in 1812 at any cost nor did he ever support any idea of breaking up the Union as some sour New England Federalists had proposed. The Union was still the "rock of our salvation."[12] Such an unthinkable split might result in foreign influence being enlarged, and he had always hated "foreigners," as he had once even unhappily labeled Albert Gallatin.[13]

Adams's dislike of Alexander Hamilton went much deeper than his criticism of Jefferson. The latter might love a "sweetness of style" and favor "public opinion,"[14] but Hamilton was nothing but an "intriguer." Both John and Abigail had disliked him for years. Adams thought that Hamilton had opposed him from the moment of his return to America. In a "dark and insidious" manner this "intriguer" had laid schemes in secret against him, and "like the worm at the root of the peach" had labored for twelve years "underground and in darkness, to girdle the root."[15]

Some of Adams's hatred for Hamilton may be ascribed to simple envy and to a love of picturesque language. However, he thought that Hamilton had never been a true Revolutionary character like himself—prior to 1775 that is.[16] Criticism of Hamilton primarily related to Adams's years of Presidency when Hamilton, apparently with some reason, had thought of himself as the leading Federalist and to what Adams considered to have been downright "treachery" on the part of Hamilton's friends in the Cabinet. Hamilton's "letter" in 1800 had been the ultimate proof of his duplicity. He was a creature in a "delirium of ambition" and simply opposed anyone who stood in his way, Adams wrote.

Adams even attacked Hamilton's background and character, saying that good wine in good company made this "bastard brat of a Scotch pedlar" act "silly," and that his vanity made him susceptible to flattery by "Tories." The latter had "puffed" up Washington only because they wanted to raise up Hamilton.[17] Adams did not add—as he might very well have—that Hamilton, like Washington, had been a military figure during the American Revolution, and a one-time aide de camp of Washington as well as his Secretary of the Treasury.

Despite his realistic attitude, when abroad, that the war had to be won at home,[18] John Adams never would admit the full role of military men in the American Revolution, always fearing a "man on horseback"; nor, unlike Hamilton, was he ever to see the necessity for the economic changes that had accompanied the war.[19] All men should have been as "pure" as himself, he had always thought. His self-righteousness and explosiveness were never as pronounced as in his early years of "retirement."

His explosiveness is especially apparent in his angry exchange of letters with Mercy Otis Warren in 1807, following the publication of her three-volume *History of the Rise, Progress, and Termination of the American Revolution, Interspersed With Biographical, Political, and Moral Observations.*[20] It should be remembered that this sister of James Otis, Jr. had once been a dear friend and neighbor of the Adamses, as had her deceased husband, General James Warren; that she had been an outspoken Whig before the American Revolution and a writer of satirical plays about the local "Tories"; and that she was a feminist with strong feelings. Her husband, a one-time political ally of John Adams, had fallen into hard times in later years; but his sympathy for Shays Rebellion had never set well with Adams, who also remembered that the Warrens, through the General's wife, had tried to get a Federal appointment from him.

The Adams-Warren correspondence of 1807[21] is painful to dwell upon: two old friends being turned into enemies. Mrs. Warren even thought Adams's long letters hypocritical because they were written "in the spirit of friendship."[22] In her last letter she merely described herself as one in whose bosom respect and affection had once existed. Even if their reconciliation did later occur (through the good offices of Elbridge Gerry), Adams must have forfeited much of her respect. Perhaps he had simply worn her out, as has been suggested; but in any case it was a sad epistolary performance. Her most charitable comment was that his "nerves" had never been "wound up by the same key."[23] She accused him of always having said different things at different times, even before 1776.

Curiously, her last charge provided something of a defense of John Adams. Mercy Warren had apparently never appreciated his ambivalent character. If he had said different things at different times even before 1776, he must always have been a much more complicated man than she could appreciate. True, he had always defended the right to "liberty" in America like the "Britannic Statesman" he was, but as early as 1766, in his "Clarendon" articles, he had called the British Constitution a mixture; in his oration to the Town of Braintree in 1772 had said that a "mixed" government is best; and in the Revolutionary Congress in 1776, on the subject of a new government, had said that a powerful executive would be necessary to prevent a "flood of democracy" from overwhelming the country.[24] No doubt his foreign experience had had some influence (she had never been abroad, herself); but if he had never been "wound up by the same key," this must have meant something about John Adams that she had never understood at all.

John Adams for his part simply denied that he had forgotten the principles of the American Revolution, as she accused him of doing. These had been as various as the thirteen states themselves and as diversified as the individuals concerned, he said.[25] The "only object" of the Revolution had been opposition to the unlimited authority of Parliament, not for any new form of government.[26] (Americans had apparently been driven into independence.) The best government for America had always been republican but "mixed," with all branches independent to prevent tyranny, as he said he had always maintained.

It is possible that Mercy Warren had never understood what John Adams had thought the American Revolution to be all about, politically, nor of the inevitability of parties developing after the Revolution any more than he understood this, himself. She now appeared to him an old Tom Paine. She seemed to think that his "removal" from the Presidency by "the free suffrage of a majority of the people" in 1800 was synonymous with her charge that "a large portion" of Americans had agreed with her.[27] The accuracy of such a charge Adams would have vehemently denied (as would any historian), even if he had fully comprehended what had happened in the Electoral College in 1800 because of "party" organization. She had appealed to "the ocean of public opinion" in publishing her work, but all he could hope for was "fame," which she correctly accused him of craving.[28]

The Adams-Warren affair is regretable, of course, and Adams's explosiveness had led to some sharp language; but it is intellectually as well as in human terms understandable. He had been correct in the larger sense, even if he had said that a man "never looks so silly as when he is talking or writing concerning himself." He had even once declared that he was "sorry" that she had "necessitated" his "fatiguing" her with "tedious" letters.[29] Her charges of his "meanness" and "malignancy" in trying to "blast" a work which "judges of literary merit" had spoken well of, insulting to "a woman of my age and standing in society," and her final charge of his "rancor, indecency, and vulgarism,"[30] are simply angry expressions of her own. She was as full of words as he was, himself.

In addition to being explosive and "silly," John Adams in early "retirement" was indeed to express jealousy: that fame seemed to be given to other people than to himself. His freewheeling correspondence with Dr. Benjamin Rush from 1805 to 1813 was to reveal his crowning indiscretion of writing off the cuff. His facetiousness or "little vein of satire," observable even as a young man, he said, was to show up again and again.[31]

It is ironic that it was the detested Alexander Hamilton who had coined the expression, "The love of fame, the ruling passion of the noblest minds," i.e., the goad of Americans in 1776, which has been applied by historians to a book of correspondence by Adams and Rush. Although they covered an enormous range of subjects, much of it was antiHamilton. However, both men were really concerned with another thing in particular: the tendency towards hero worship which made folklore out of Washington and others thus neglecting their own claim to fame.[32]

As these two old patriots of 1776 chewed over the past they agreed upon almost everything except a veneration for "dead" languages (which Rush opposed). They addressed each other as "My dear old Friend," "My excellent Friend," "Friend of '74," and the like. Adams summed up their thinking by saying, "These puffers, Rush, are the only killers of scandal. Washington, Franklin—I will go no farther at present—killed all scandal by puffers. You and I have never employed them, and therefore scandal has prevailed against us. . . ."[33] His particular brand of anticlericalism and hatred of Hamilton is shown in his thought that "The pious and virtuous Hamilton, in 1790, began to teach our nation Christianity and to commission his fellows to cry down Jefferson and Madison as atheists in league with the French nation. Your 'British Federalists' and your 'Tory Federalists' [Rush had mentioned these as well as "American Federalists"] instantly joined in the clamor. Their newspapers and their pulpits, at least in New England, have resounded with these denunciations for many years."[34]

The fascinating Adams-Rush correspondence has deeply influenced modern historical thought. Of course the letters are of inestimable value in themselves. Even though the good Doctor had once thought Adams a "monarchist," Adams as President had befriended Rush with a badly needed appointment regardless of his political opinions and because Rush was an "old Whig," and there was no political bar between them now.

Their only difference evoked a comment by Adams that is worthy of becoming a classic of humor. "Mrs. Adams says she is willing you should discredit Greek and Latin because it will destroy the foundation of all the pretentions of the gentlemen to superiority over the ladies and restore liberty, equality, and fraternity between the sexes. What does Mrs. Rush think of this?"[35] (Abigail had always had to consult her husband or one of her sons when dealing with "dead" languages.)

John Adams never wrote a kindlier letter than when he heard of Rush's death in 1813. He told the grieving widow, "There is not a man out of my own family remaining in the world in whom I had so much confidence, for whom I felt so tender an affection, and whose friendship was so essential to my happiness. My loss and my sensibility of it can bear no proportion, however, to yours. . . ."[36]

One of the fruits of John Adams's correspondence with Rush was the healing of the old breach with Jefferson, which Rush had urged insistently. Since both men had professed affection for the other, he had urged each to write the other. Perhaps Adams in 1811 characterized old political differences as well as anyone has ever characterized them when he facetiously wrote, "Jefferson and Rush were for liberty and straight hair. I thought curled hair was as republican as straight."[37]

If John Adams was sometimes frivolous or facetious in writing Rush, it was in pure anger that he sent a mass of letters to the Boston *Patriot* in 1809-1812, because of "pro-French" charges. These deal primarily with the years of his Presidency and his old complaints against Hamilton, but also with his earlier experiences in Holland (where Mercy Warren had said he had enjoyed himself). About three quarters of these communications were subsequently collected in a book and some were reprinted by Charles Francis Adams in appendices to the first and ninth volume of the *Works*. Adams's career in Holland and during his Presidency are not dealt with either in his diary or in his formal *Autobiography*.[38]

In the *Autobiography* one can find Adams's opinions about men and events in the early years—at least as he remembered them for he did not consult his diary at first. This major effort he made between 1802 and 1807, other attempts at "autobiography" having been suspended for one reason or another.

Unfortunately it is hard to believe everything any man in "retirement" says, especially by such an opinionated person as John Adams. An old man may be correct in his judgments, but history is usually made by younger men and is frequently recorded in "diaries," such as John Adams had once kept.

Despite the esteemed privacy of his home life, the "Old Man" (the term is used affectionately, and only because he had been so dubbed earlier and sometimes used it himself) continued to be absorbed in politics, like all Americans both then and since. Party success seemed to him to be like a game of "leapfrog," with an alternation between the "ins" and the "outs." His total correspondence, including that with Dr. Rush, must have been enormous. Some of it has been put into books. The founder of a "writing family," he expended unbelievable quantities of energy for his descendants to match. Every subject under the sun came under caustic examination; his language was uniformly colorful and full of familiar biblical references, as to the "Wilderness," the "Promised Land," the "Lord's Anointed," and so forth.

A last retort in this period, on the subject of political theory, was his answer in thirty-three letters in 1814 to John Taylor of Caroline, Virginia, whose *Inquiry into the Principles and Policy of Government* had recently appeared and was largely an attack on Adams's old *Defence.* Taylor had rejected Adams's distinction between the one, the few, and the many, but the "Old Man" simply insisted on what he had always said: That there is a "natural" aristocracy in mankind which poor education can make even worse.[39]

About Adams's life in Quincy during his retirement, little is known. Scholars have not yet fully investigated the problem.[40] The "Old Man" enjoyed physical labor although most of the farm work was done by hired hands. He rejoiced in the size of his manure pile and drank a quart of hard cider before eating a hearty New England breakfast. He not only wrote voluminously but read a good deal (although he seemed to have read everything, already), sometimes in the garden.

Little is known about Abigail in these years either, beyond her graciousness and her supervision of a large household of descendants and servants, and no doubt the supervision of her opinionated if lovable husband.[41] The Adamses invariably had boiled cornmeal to start their dinner before the meat course, but Abigail or her niece did the carving when that came around. John conversed. The country-like place was to appear quite primitive to such a dainty person as the wife of John Quincy Adams, when she made her first visit there in 1801. Luckily, "The Old Gentleman" took an immediate liking to his new daughter-in-law, even if Abigail had her reservations.[42]

CHAPTER 10

Hail and Farewell

"It can clip no longer"

THE last ten years of John Adams's life, beginning at the age of eighty, were mostly vigorous ones; they seem to have been "more of the same." He was never in senility, for his mind remained clear to the last. If it is only in childhood or "second childhood" that one sees things in the round, then John Adams never saw things in their entirety because he never had much of a "second childhood." His ideas remained about the same. He "mellowed" very little, although he did sometimes forget some disagreeable things and romanticized occasionally.

His physical condition also remained about the same, until 1824 or so. He had long since lost some teeth and had complained for many years of a "quiveration," perhaps palsy, in his hand when trying to write (and most of his "writing" after 1818 seems to have been dictated); but at least he avoided the dreaded, miserable condition that had marked down Sam Adams in later years.[1] He even smoked a cigar after dinner apparently to the very end, and Gilbert Stuart caught some of the old fire in the last portrait he painted in 1823-24. The artist, perhaps something of a wag, is said to have remarked that it was a good likeness but that the "Old Man" looked as if he were about to sneeze.[2]

It is true that Adams in older age sometimes acted pompously, like a senior citizen become a sage, but this was an old habit and pomposity can always be excused in the elderly. He was also to prove that the old can understand the young (having once been young themselves), for the Adams household remained full of young people in whom he is said to have continued to delight.[3] Whether the young ever understand the old is more debatable (and on this the Adams record is more or less silent, although grandsons and nieces sometimes read to the "Old Man" and took dictation). Most of the work at the "Old House" was done by maids, doubtless under the supervision of Louisa Smith, a self-effacing spinster and niece of Abigail and a long and dear resident in the household.

Adams had frequently spoken of his own approach to death—he had always worried about his health and had frequently predicted an early demise—but the idea of a resurrection became more of a reality in his last years. Although he did not believe in the tenets of any particular church he had always thought of himself as a deeply religious man.

The years 1813-1815 must have made a great dividing line in the lives of John and Abigail Adams. Daughter Nabby died in 1813 (having been operated on for cancer several years before), and so did John's beloved old correspondent, Benjamin Rush of Philadelphia. The year 1814 saw the passing of several old political friends, notably Elbridge Gerry, and of Mercy Otis Warren of Plymouth. Abigail lost her only remaining sister, Eliza, in 1815; and Colonel Smith, the husband of Nabby, died that same year, as did a life-long friend and business agent, Cousin Dr. Cotton Tufts.[4]

The final and greatest loss for John Adams was to be the death of Abigail in late 1818, his wife of fifty-four years, and what he was to write after that may express the religious acceptance that was steadily growing upon him: "The bitterness of death is past."[5]

The resounding vigor of John Adams until about 1824 is amazing. He suffered not only because of death and rheumatism and his old "quiveration," but because of a complete loss of teeth. The portrait by Morse in 1816 shows this plainly, as does the portrait by Stuart of 1823-24 and as does the life mask taken by Browère about that time. Even Abigail must sometimes have suffered along these lines, if the silhouette which still hangs in the White House is any kind of clue.[6]

Adams's reconciliation with Thomas Jefferson, resulting from Rush's efforts, had led to a correspondence that throws considerable light on his *credo*. Although he never formally wrote out his social and political philosophy, he obviously believed in some of the ideas of Alexander Pope, and in history, humanism, religion, and of course in the social fabric of New England. Quite opposite in viewpoint was his contemporary from Virginia, who revered Condorcet and "theories." Even when Jefferson finally agreed about the possibility of inequality existing even in America—a natural aristocracy and an artificial one, the first moral and the latter immoral—the Stoic Adams refused to

concede that this was enough. One kind of aristocracy is as corrupt as
the other, he thought. Social influence—especially wealth—and a
lack of good education could make the situation even worse. He
congratulated Jefferson on his interest in the University of Virginia.[7]

Jefferson has been called "The Apostle of Americanism" and
Adams has not, but the latter did not believe in "entangling
alliances" with foreign nations, either, and had once even thought
that Jefferson had stolen his thunder in this respect. It was not really
America *versus* Europe, it was theory *versus* history, as Adams saw
it. Of course, there was a degree of isolationism about the thinking of
both men, appropriate to what the eighteenth century had taught.

It was the optimistic Jefferson who believed in "progress" and in
what was later called "Manifest Destiny," whereas Adams always saw
man from the viewpoint of a moralist: as a creature of passions and
vices and appetites (he did not mention sex) as recorded in all human
history. The idea that man was perfectible was "mischievous
nonsense." Americans were no different from any other people, he
thought. Even American politicians might become as ambitious and
corrupt as diplomats of the Old Régime. He did not dislike his
fellowmen—he was no reactionary—he merely "pitied" them, he
said.[8]

On the subject of morality Adams and Jefferson agreed, and both
scorned ecclesiastical usurpations, but on the subject of death there
was something of a difference between them. Jefferson once spoke of
a "meeting" with lost friends after death but he spoke rather
doubtfully (perhaps even hypocritically, although he can be forgiven
under the circumstances), whereas Adams always refused to be
rationalistic about religion in general and certainly about a future
state. He had half-humorously warned Jefferson in 1817 to "TRUST
IN GOD," and later was sure that all men are "by nature religious
creatures." He thought that Jesus may have taught that a future state
is a "social state" when Jesus had promised to prepare places in His
Father's house of many mansions, but that is about as far as Adams's
own vision went, and it was a religious vision. It may be observed that
he did not identify the Kingdom of God in Heaven with the Kingdom
of God on Earth, as it is sometimes said the old Puritans had intended. If true, this would have made Jefferson the true heir of the
Puritans rather than Adams himself; but it is a dubious point.[9]

Another difference between the two men was John Adams's
general lack of interest in aesthetics. As he once wrote Jefferson, it is
harder to be a law-giver than an architect or painter; and he seems to

have had little interest in music as such, unlike Jefferson the violinist. He had heard of Handel, of course, and sometimes listened to ladies perform on the pianoforte or spinet, and had enjoyed songs as a young man, but a century of remarkable musical achievement seems to have passed him by.[10]

As for past politics and new problems, Adams's thinking after 1818, while always honest, became more emphatic than ever. This is sometimes confusing to historians since they often fail to recognize that old people are likely to simplify things. There was no confusion in Adams's own mind, however, although "very little" could be expected at his age, he once warned.[11] He increasingly identified the American Revolution with a Massachusetts view, and, like the "Tories," with the role originally played there by James Otis, Jr., in opposition to the idea that it was Patrick Henry of Virginia who had given the first impetus towards independence. Adams praised Otis, especially in connection with the Writs of Assistance in 1760—Otis had been like a "flame"—for having laid the foundation.[12]

The American colonists had always wanted independence of Parliament in "internal taxation" and "internal policy," Adams said, but there never had been much of "a desire of independence of the crown" before the Revolution, or from general regulation of commerce impartially treated throughout the empire. Identifying the American Revolution with himself, he declared that there had never been a moment when he would not have "given every thing" for a restoration to things as they had been before the contest began providing there could have been any guarantee of their continuance. He had always "dreaded" the Revolution as "fraught with ruin to me and my family," as he said had proved to be more or less the case.[13]

With the Missouri question looming on the horizon, Adams asserted in 1819 that the trade in slaves from Africa had always been infamous, and that he himself had never owned any kind of slave even when that practice had been socially acceptable. Humanity required the extirpation of slavery, but this should be done with "prudence."[14]

The American Indians were also held in Adams's compassion in old age. Of course Indians were "savages" but they had had rights; he could not see how they "could have been treated with more equity or humanity than they have been in general in North America." England, on the other hand, had always treated Indian claims abominably in colonial times taking dominion over their land. Hutchinson in his *History* had shown little consideration for the suffering colonists in the Indian Wars as had been commonly noticed at the time,

Adams said. Anyway, it was all a matter of religious bigotry he was sure, on the part of the Indians as well as on the part of Englishmen, like that "pious tyrant," Archbishop Laud.[15]

The Golden Rule must have come to play a large part in Adams's thinking about political matters. He defined liberty in 1819 as "a power to do as we would be done by."[16]

In Adams's correspondence with William Tudor of Boston, beginning in early 1818, he really let himself go about James Otis, Jr., even while lamenting Otis's later "indecision and inconsistency." Tudor intended to write a biography of Otis. As the "Old Man" saw it, Otis and others had merely been the "awakeners and revivers" of the principles that had marked American colonization. Adams had not agreed with Otis's views about the Empire in 1768, having had long thought, he once said, that Parliament had never had any right to legislate for America "in any case whatever"; he was weary of dealing with such "trash."[17] (Theoretically the whole Revolution in Massachusetts had depended on whether Otis had been in his right mind in 1768.) The "oily brush" of Sam Adams could be seen in the "collation" of Otis's words. (The "arrangement of words" is more important than accuracy in some writers, John Adams asserted, and "woe to the Writer" who neglects it.) It was sad that "any American should still doubt the equity and wisdom" of the decision which "God and the world" had made about the outcome of the American Revolution.[18]

It is impressive that in one of Adams's last letters to Tudor, in 1819, he could still honestly acknowledge his old criticism of Otis about the Empire and the authority of the High Court of Parliament; but he thought that the "rough cast" of Otis had even then been subject to the "burnish and polish" of Sam Adams, who drew his authority from "the people."[19]

Perhaps Adams was right, as a Massachusetts man, in saying that James Otis, Jr. was the real founder of the American Revolution; or, perhaps, he should have said, Sam Adams; or, perhaps, himself. The American Revolution in Massachusetts must have had various spokesmen as it snowballed along.

In old age, Adams was increasingly sure that he had always advocated a union of all America. He continued to be sceptical of "democratic" and "peace" organizations, for one thing because he doubted that Americans were a peace loving people.[20] He also continued to lament the advent of "materialism." He apparently had some hopes for the Middle West as a result of the opening of the Erie

Canal, in commemoration of which he was to receive a medal in 1826.

The death of his neighbor and only remaining brother, Peter, ocurred in 1823. Little seems to be known about Peter, except that as a boy he had once listened in on a family spat, that he was "always impish," and that he had grown hard of hearing and poor of seeing. He had loudly and jokingly referred to Brother John as "Moses" at a town meeting.[21]

Beginning the next year John Adams became increasingly frail in a physical way. He first gave up horseback riding, and then his long daily walks. He would fall down after walking a hundred rods. He began to think of himself like an old clock, with all its parts worn out until it could "clip no longer."[22]

His reading in the garden in the afternoons was soon given up completely, although he continued to use his chair in the study. The picture of old "Juno" wagging her tail at the approach of a visitor while the "Old Man" smoked his pipe, was apparently a thing of the past. (Incidentally, this is one of the few references to "pets" in the John Adams saga.)

The classics had always been dear to John Adams, and he followed the reading of his grandsons as they became acquainted with them. One marvels that he was able to read so much. He even enjoyed Scott's historical romances when they began to come out in serial form, and these are ponderous things. He also enjoyed the early sea stories of Cooper, and the vigorous poetry of Byron.[23] History, especially that of New England, and travel books, such as he had always loved, were also a part of his intellectual fare. This old age love of the novels of Sir Walter Scott is in particular most revealing. Apparently the romanticizing of the nineteenth century had already begun.

Adams's love of old New England continued to be especially marked. In 1822 he was to see that "the whole history of America" had exhibited a "uniform, general tenor of character for intelligence, integrity, patience, fortitude, and public spirit." It was not the disinterestedness of the Washingtons and Hancocks which deserved the credit, he thought, but the settlers, themselves. One generation had little reason to boast over another, he said.[24]

The career of his dutiful and hard working eldest son, John Quincy Adams, was of tremendous satisfaction throughout these later years. When John Quincy had been made Secretary of State by President Monroe, in 1817, both John and Abigail were enormously pleased; and the son's eventual election to the Presidency in 1825 was the father's last great joy. It had been achieved at the expense of the popularity of General Jackson whom the "Old Man" is said to have much admired but who was not to be compared to Adams's own brilliant son.

The last public act of John Adams was to attend the Massachusetts Constitutional Convention in Boston in 1821, to consider revising the old frame that he had principally engineered in 1779. There he opposed the idea of universal suffrage, attacking unlimited democracy in favor of property qualifications which he had always advocated as a necessity for responsibility in government. He also opposed that provision which gave the state the right to recognize different modes of religious worship (somewhat in the spirit of religious liberty which Jefferson had advanced in Virginia years before). Sad to relate, when both ideas were gently put aside John Adams acquiesced, publicly at least. After all, he was tired; the long sessions of the Convention had wearied him.[25]

John Adams's last written words seem to have been, "Long and lasting prosperity to the City and State of New York!" The ninety year old man had been invited to attend a fiftieth year celebration of the signing of the Declaration of Independence there, just as Thomas Jefferson had been invited to attend a similar celebration in Washington, D.C. Of course neither man could go.

Perhaps the most fascinating thing about John Adams is that he should have died that day, the Fourth of July, 1826, exactly fifty years after the Declaration had been formally adopted and on the very same day that Jefferson died. The two old associates of 1776 had finally been united, not only by correspondence in old age but by death itself.

A sense of awe, even of religious awe, seems to have swept the country as the news of their passing on that day was bruited about. A divine providence seemed to have been back of everything in American history, especially the American Revolution. Jefferson would have been appalled by the religious interpretation (so different from his old rationalistic ideas), unless indeed he considered himself an instrument of divine providence as Adams in old age apparently considered himself to have been. Perhaps the nineteenth century was more religious than the eighteenth, but in any case it was soon overwhelmed by a welter of patriotic prophesy and romanticizing. The two old men had contributed to this in the manner of their passing.

It is difficult to appreciate John Adams's achievement in the American Revolutionary era, not only because two hundred years have passed, but because he was a builder of governments while speculation about the nature of government has long since gone out of vogue.

His comments should be taken seriously even if he sometimes does sound amusing and pompous. If his cutting remarks about men and events are seen today as humorous, and he himself as something of a "character," that may be because our twentieth century finds its amusement primarily in personality traits and no longer believes in the importance of egos, which in John Adams's case was huge.

John Adams was a great man in spite of everything because of his ambivalent nature. He revered religious teaching even if he did cast aside all religious tenets. He nurtured ministerial "truth" even if he did favor the "evidence" of law. He craved higher learning even if he enjoyed a farmer's life. He wrote on both sides of the question in the "Ploughjogger" controversy in 1763. He liked some of the gentry even if he did favor "the people." He was an American patriot even if he was a "Britannic Statesman." He was a good republican even if he did have doubts about "democracy" and did favor "mixed" government. He was an isolationist even if he did appreciate European affairs. He favored a "model" treaty although he did accept the French Alliance. He liked the British form of government even if he did enjoy French cooking. He favored public virtue even if he did recognize the necessity for self-interest. He was in favor of adopting the Constitution of the United States even if his eldest son at first opposed it. The list is almost endless. His ambivalence always showed, except when he lost his temper and became opinionated.

The description of John Adams as given by his grandson is worthy of recall, although the subject does rather resemble Mr. Pickwick.

He was, Charles Francis Adams tells us, not tall but of a stout, well-knit frame, his head large and round, with a wide forehead and extended eyebrows, and a tendency towards corpulence as he grew older. His eye was "mild and benignant, perhaps even humorous, when he was free from emotion, but when excited, it fully expressed the vehemence of the spirit that stirred within." He delighted in social conversation, in which he sometimes engaged in what he called "rhodomontade." His affections towards his relatives, while "warm," were "not habitually demonstrated." His anger when aroused— especially because of wrongdoing, when his vehemence sometimes made him overbearing and unjust—was terrible to behold, but it left no malevolence behind. He hated cant. He had little respect for the status of persons. "Ambitious in one sense he certainly was," but it was not mere "aspiration for place or power." He loved to excel and craved an honorable fame "that stirred him to exult in the rewards of popular favor," but he never changed his mind because of a disagreeable truth.

In addition, he had fortunately been married for fifty-four years to a most remarkable woman, and they had had a son who had filled his highest expectations.[26]

For the memory of John Adams, we can all be thankful.

Notes and References

1. See the footnote comments in the *Diary and Autobiography of John Adams*, L. H. Butterfield, ed., L. C. Faber and W. D. Garrett, asst. eds. (4 vols., Cambridge, 1961, reissued in paperback, New York, 1964), I, 168n, III, 257n., hereafter referred to as *Diary and Autobiography*. This is the latest edition of the Diary originally edited by Charles Francis Adams, with autobiographical passages and inserts, in volumes two and three of the *Works of John Adams, Second President of the United States: with a Life of the Author* . . . (10 vols., Boston, 1856), hereafter referred to as *Works*.

2. On this whole subject, see Herbert Leventhal, *In the Shadow of the Enlightenment: Occultism and Renaissance Science in Eighteenth-Century America* (New York, 1976), *passim*.

3. *Diary and Autobiography,* III, 256. Part One of Adams's *Auto-biography* begins in the third volume of this work on page 253. See also his letter of 1809, in *Works,* IX, 610ff.

4. *Diary and Autobiography,* I. 79, under entry of March 14, 1759. For Adams's account of an earlier family spat, see *Ibid.,* I, 65, which is worth mentioning here because it throws light on Adams's parents as well as upon himself—and because it is an early example of what Charles Francis Adams saw fit to exclude when editing his grandfather's works.

5. *Diary and Autobiography,* III, 256n, referring to a letter written in 1820. *Works,* IX, 612, refers to his later estimate of his stature.

6. Page Smith, *John Adams* (2 vols., New York, 1962), I, 57, 58, hereafter referred to as Smith, *Adams.*

7. *Diary and Autobiography,* III, 256, 257. Catherine Drinker Bowen, *John Adams and the American Revolution* (Boston, 1949) p. 13. This work, hereafter referred to as Bowen, *Adams,* though highly imaginative, is based on thorough research and gives a wealth of detailed information.

8. Charles Francis Adams (Jr.), *Three Episodes of Massachusetts History* (2 vols., revised, copyright 1892, reissued in New York, 1965), II, 732ff., hereafter referred to as Adams, *Three Episodes.* See also John Adams's remark in *Works,* IX, 637.

9. Briant is discussed in Adams, *Three Episodes,* II, 636ff. See also Gilbert Chinard, *Honest John Adams* (Boston, 1933), pp. 17-18, hereafter referred to as Chinard, *Adams.* This work is especially important not only

because of its thoughtful observations, but because Chinard had earlier written a life of Jefferson: *Thomas Jefferson, the Apostle of Americanism* (Boston, 1929).

10. *Diary and Autobiography*, III, 253.

11. Some of these ideas began quite early. See Adams's statement in old age (1820), in *Works*, X, 389, 390.

12. Adams, *Three Episodes*, II, 822ff.

13. *Ibid.*, esp. p. 796 and also p. 733. See also Smith, *Adams*, I, 3, and Adams, *Three Episodes*, II, 796, 797.

14. John Adams wrote years later that Episcopacy in Quincy had made it a focus of "bigotry, intrigue, intolerance, and persecution": *Works*, X, 187. See also Adams, *Three Episodes*, II, 629ff., esp. 632.

15. See Adams's recollection in *Works*, IX, 591. Bowen, *Adams*, Ch. I, makes a good deal of this in the boy's experience.

16. *Diary and Autobiography*, III, 257 and 258n.

17. *Works*, X, 19.

18. Boston *Evening-Post*, Sept. 5, 1763.

19. Cf. *Diary and Autobiography*, I, 12n. See also the last chapter of this work.

20. *Ibid.*, III, 260.

21. *Ibid.*, pp. 257, 258.

22. *Ibid.*, p. 262. See also Adams's recollection in 1813, in *The Spur of Fame, Dialogues of John Adams and Benjamin Rush, 1805-1813* (John A. Schutz and Douglass Adair, eds., The Huntington Library, San Marino, 1966), pp. 239, 262, hereafter referred to as *Spur of Fame*.

23. *Diary and Autobiography*, III, p. 259.

Chapter Two

1. This description and what follows is based principally on Bowen, *Adams*, p. 62 and ff. See also, *Spur of Fame*, p. 262, for Adams's remembrance in old age, about his early life, education, etc.

2. *Ibid.*, p. 79.

3. *Diary and Autobiography*, III, 261.

4. See *Works*, IX, 613; also *The Earliest Diary of John Adams* (Cambridge, 1966), p. 34, hereafter referred to as *Earliest Diary*.

5. *Earliest Diary*, p. 51n.

6. *Ibid.*, p. 50n.

7. See the *Harvard Magazine* for March-April, 1978, which has Copley's portrait of Holyoke on the cover.

8. *Cf.* Bowen, *Adams*, p. 75 and ff; also Smith, *Adams*, I, 20.

9. On Hancock, see *Works*, X, 259. Adams apparently had also known Hannah Quincy as a girl in Braintree: Bowen, *Adams*, p. 180.

10. See Adams's recollection in old age, *Diary and Autobiography*, III, 262, 263.

11. See Bowen, *Adams*, p. 97ff., especially for "Uncle Eb."

12. *Earliest Diary*, p. 33.

13. *Ibid.*, pp. 36, 37.

14. Smith, *Adams*, I, 24. Chinard, *Adams*, p. 12, says that Adams's years at Harvard could not have been "particularly pleasant."

15. *Earliest Diary*, p. 37; *Diary and Autobiography*, III, 265.

16. *Diary and Autobiography*, III, 266, 269, 270.

17. *Ibid.*, p. 264. See especially the diary entry under August 25, 1756, *Diary and Autobiography*, I, 44 and footnotes on page 45. See also *Works*, IX, 611.

18. *Diary and Autobiography*, I, pp. 18, 20, 22, 23, 25, 28, 32, 60ff., etc. Chinard, *Adams*, p. 14, speaks about the later diary references to the "starry heavens."

19. *Ibid.*, p. 10 and note, also p. 108.

20. *Ibid.*, p. 43.

21. *Works*, IX, 630.

22. This is a curious episode although Chinard, *Adams*, pp. 29, 30, practically ignores it. Compare Adams's account in *Diary and Autobiography*, I, 56, with his recollection in old age, *ibid.*, III, 270ff. Bowen, *Adams*, p. 164 and esp. p. 177ff. makes a great deal of this episode, especially about Prat's manner.

23. On Betsy, see *Earliest Diary*, pp. 14, 91, and 92n.

24. This is also a knotty problem because of Adams's later emphasis in *Works*, IX, 591, 612, etc. Chinard, *Adams*, pp. 23-25, deals with this problem in proper perspective.

25. On his "milk" diet, see *Diary and Autobiography*, III, 269, and his comment in 1813 in *Works*, X, 68. On Adams's intermittent illnesses, his revolt against his father's authority and hence against all authority, and psychological explanations for all this, see Peter Shaw, *The Character of John Adams* (Chapel Hill, 1976), *passim*, esp. pp. 39, 51n (on the father image in "Clarendon"), 65n. This work is hereafter referred to as Shaw, *Adams*.

Chapter Three

1. On Adams as a lawyer, see the Introduction to *The Legal Papers of John Adams*, K. Wroth and H. Zobel, eds. (3 vols., Cambridge, 1968), I, iii ff., hereafter referred to as *Legal Papers*. On Adams's early reading, see *ibid.*, I, xxxvi, xli; *Diary and Autobiography*, I, 44ff., 72, 82, 173, etc.; *Works*, I, 46; Bowen, *Adams*, p. 192.

2. See footnotes 11, 19, and 20, below.

3. See footnotes 6, 7, and 8, below.

4. Adams, *Three Episodes*, II, 783ff., esp. 785ff; *Diary and Autobiography*, I, 130 and 130n., 137, III, 277; *Works*, II, 58n.; Chinard, *Adams*, p. 39.

5. See *Diary and Autobiography,* I, esp. 88 about buying a "Husbandmans Place Book," and ff.

6. On Hannah, or "O" or "Orlinda" or "Olinda," see *ibid.,* I, li; *Earliest Diary,* pp. 12, 13, 69, 70, 81n; also Bowen, *Adams,* pp. 102, 187, etc.

7. *Diary and Autobiography,* I, 176, 177.

8. On Cranch, see *ibid.,* I, 114; also *Earliest Diary,* 12, 13, 81n.

9. See my "The Strange Pause in John Adams's Diary," in *Toward a New View of America* (New York, 1977) esp. pp. 22, 23, 26, and 31 notes 8 and 17; hereafter referred to as East, "Strange Pause in John Adams's Diary." See also *Works,* I, 61. The most recent study of Sewall is Carol Berkin, *Jonathan Sewall, Odyssey of an American Loyalist* (New York, 1974). On page 27 of this work reference is made to Sewall's appointment as a Justice of the Peace for Middlesex County, his commission dated November 20, 1761.

10. See Bowen, *Adams,* p. 163. See also the use of "our" and "we" in his critical but unpublished remarks in *Diary and Autobiography,* I, 186.

11. The instances are innumerable: see *Diary and Autobiography,* I, 167, 168, 190, 193, 221, 242. See also footnotes 19 and 20, below.

12. *Ibid.,* lxxvii, pp. 24, 25, 42, 78, 82, 83, 84, 95, 96, etc.

13. *Ibid.,* p. 236.

14. According to his eldest son, John Quincy Adams: *Works,* I, 62. See also the Introduction to the *Legal Papers,* I.

15. *Diary and Autobiography,* I, 53, 80, 95, 100, 118, 123, 168, etc.

16. *Ibid.,* pp. 118, 168, 171, 200.

17. *Ibid.,* pp. 168, 217, 229.

18. *Ibid.,* p. 186.

19. *Ibid.,* pp. 190, 204.

20. *Ibid.,* p. 193.

21. *Ibid.,* pp. 37, 167.

22. *Ibid.,* p. 153.

23. *Ibid.,* pp. 248, 250n; also East, "Strange Pause in John Adams's Diary," *passim.* Adams said in 1816 that the "separation of parties" did not begin until 1766: *Works,* X, 197, but the "contest" began earlier, apparently: *Diary and Autobiography,* II, 95.

24. *Diary and Autobiography,* I, 234, 235.

25. See *Works,* X, 194ff. for Adams's remembrance in old age. On Leonard's authorship of "Massachusettensis," see *Diary and Autobiography,* II, 161n, and especially *Adams Family Correspondence,* (L. H. Butterfield, ed., W. D. Garrett, assoc. ed., M. E. Sprague, asst. ed. for the first two volumes, L. H. Butterfield and Marc Friedlaender, eds., for the third and fourth volumes, Cambridge, 1965-1973, covering the years through 1782), I, 181n. This work is hereafter referred to as *Adams Family Correspondence.*

26. On Prat, for remembrance, see *Works,* X, 242, and for contemporary thought, *Diary and Autobiography,* I, 309; on Willard, *Diary and Autobiography,* III, 266. See also East, "Strange Pause in John Adams's Diary," p. 25 and p. 32 note 25.

27. See *Works,* I, 61ff. for an account by his eldest son. Adams himself wrote in 1811 that Abigail was a daughter of the clergyman said by his fellow clergymen to be the "richest" in the Province: *The Spur of Fame,* p. 188.

28. Bowen, *Adams,* p. 239; Smith, *Adams,* I, 68; Chinard, *Adams,* p. 45; Janet Whitney, *Abigail Adams* (Boston, 1947), pp. 6, 20, 22, 23. See especially Charles Francis Adams (Sr.), *Familiar Letters of John Adams and His Wife Abigail Adams During the Revolution with a Memoir of Mrs. Adams* (Boston, 1875), xiv, xv, hereafter referred to as *Familiar Letters.*

29. *Adams Family Correspondence,* I, 10n, 11, 38, 50.

Chapter Four

1. See the *Diary and Autobiography,* II, 6, 11, 15, 18. Adams later claimed in his *Autobiography* having had earlier fears of popular passion misleading the people: *Ibid.,* III, 290. See discussion below, and footnotes 22, 23, 24, also below. See also *Spur of Fame,* pp. 143n, 144n.

2. *Diary and Autobiography,* II, 28, concerning his wife, children, and farm.

3. *Ibid.,* I, 74, II, 72.

4. Edmund S. and Helen M. Morgan, *The Stamp Act Crisis, Prologue to Revolution* (second ed., 1962, originally published by the North Carolina Press in 1953), p. 265ff., esp. p. 269, hereafter referred to as Morgan, *Stamp Act Crisis.*

5. See Adams's recollection in *Works,* X, 192ff. On Sewall, see *ibid.,* p. 178.

6. The phrase, "Britannic Statesman," is brilliantly employed by Randolph G. Adams, *Political Ideas of the American Revolution* (originally published in 1922, 3rd ed. with an intro. by Merrill Jensen, New York, 1958), Ch. 5, and esp. p. 113.

7. *Diary and Autobiography,* I, 238.

8. *Ibid.,* p. 312n, III, 382 for Adams's autobiographical recollection. See also Shaw, *Adams,* pp. 53, 54.

9. The *Dissertation* can be found in *Works,* III, 448ff. See also Shaw, *Adams,* p. 56.

10. The "Clarendon" articles can be found in *Works,* III, 469ff. See *ibid.,* p. 475 on "Cromwell," and p. 480 on the mixed character of the British constitution (which, Adams said, always aims at liberty) in legislative matters, and in which the "power of elections," he said, even surpasses that of the House of Commons. In executive matters, Adams argues, liberty lies only in trial by jury. On page 482 he sums up the "balance and mixture of the government" which prevents it from running into an oligarchy or aristocracy, on the one hand, as the Lords and Commons prevent it from becoming an absolute monarchy on the other. The last of the "Clarendon" articles ends (*ibid.,* p. 483) with the reflection that a man should only be tried by his peers or neighbors because they naturally wish to find him innocent, and that if a

man disputes with his neighbor, other neighbors will be "indifferent on which side the truth lies."

11. See *Works,* III, 495. In his *Diary and Autobiography,* I, 365, Adams speaks in an unpublished newspaper article of the "Lies and Slanders" of Philanthrop, and of rewards in government being given to "Vanity and folly" as a result of "Elegance, Luxury and Effemincy" instead of to "Virtue, Integrity and Ability."

12. *Legal Papers,* I, lix, lxvii. See also Chapter 3 of this work, footnote 27.

13. *Adams Family Correspondence,* I, 132n.

14. *Ibid.,* p. 131.

15. *Diary and Autobiography,* I, 333, 337.

16. *Adams Family Correspondence,* I, 58 and 59n.

17. *Diary and Autobiography,* III, 287ff., 289n.

18. *Works,* III, 501ff.

19. *Ibid.,* p. 508. For the effects of the Townshend Acts, see ibid., X, 199, as Adams remembered this in 1816 when he blamed it all on Chatham.

20. Hiller B. Zobel, "Newer Light on the Boston Massacre," *Proceedings* of the American Antiquarian Society, Vol. 7, Pt. 1 (1968), p. 119ff., esp. p. 124.

21. *Diary and Autobiography,* II, 18. See also Shaw, *Adams,* p. 58ff.

22. *Diary and Autobiography,* II, 15, 28, 35. See also Shaw, *Adams,* pp. 58, 64ff. for a psychological explanation.

23. Richard D. Brown, *Revolutionary Politics in Massachusetts, the Boston Committee of Correspondence, 1772-1774* (Copyright 1970, New York, 1976), p. 58ff., hereafter referred to as Brown, *Boston Committee of Correspondence.* See also John J. Waters, *The Otis Family in Provincial and Revolutionary Massachusetts* (Chapel Hill, 1968), *passim.*

24. *Diary and Autobiography,* II, 56ff.; see also the argument made two years later by "Novanglus" about the British constitution being a "mixture"; *Works,* IV, 118.

25. *Ibid.,* pp. 65, 66 for the "Rant" against Adams, which the latter thought Otis must apply to "2 thirds of the Town." Two years before (1770) Otis must have been more or less rational, at least in expressing his old hatred for Hutchinson which Sam Adams had carried on, and with which John Adams must surely have agreed; it fitted in with Adams's theory that all history showed that one man would eventually become a tyrant and overthrow liberty, not to mention his personal feelings about Hutchinson. On Adams's inability to say anything good about Hutchinson, even that he did not believe in "witches," see *Adams Family Correspondence,* I, 121.

26. *Ibid.,* II, 73. Adams at first told the delegation that asked him to orate that his health was too bad, that he would have nothing to do with politics, etc. The delegates then asked him for his "Reasons," and he spoke more fully.

27. The comparison with *Ivanhoe* is my own, but see H. Trevor Colbourn, *The Lamp of Experience, Whig History and the Intellectual Origins of the American Revolution* (originally published in 1965, New York, 1974), esp.

Chs. 2, 9. On Paine, see my *John Quincy Adams, the Critical Years: 1785-1794* (New York, 1962), p. 145, hereafter referred to as East, *John Quincy Adams.*

28. On the controversy with Brattle, see *Works,* III, 513ff. For the threatened loss of judges' independence, etc., at a later date, see *Diary and Autobiography,* III, 298.

Chapter Five

1. *Diary and Autobiography,* I, 363, but he also said that the interest of the age and of posterity sometimes made it necessary to speak out publicly. This "virtue" of prudence (or self-interest or selfishness) he later (1807) identified with "Tories": *Spur of Fame,* p. 90, and he also distinguished between "prudence" and "cowardice" (p. 91).

2. *Ibid.,* II, 80, 81, 85.

3. Brown, *Boston Committee of Correspondence,* pp. 164, 194, although John Adams was "sympathetic." On Samuel Adams, see also Stephen E. Paterson, *Political Parties in Revolutionary Massachusetts* (Madison, 1973), pp. 57, 58.

4. See his statement in 1815 in *Works,* X, 196. The true history of the United States could never be written until the papers of the Committees of Correspondence are discovered, he said.

5. See *The British in Boston, Being the Diary of Lieutenant John Barker of the King's Own Regiment from November 15, 1774 to May 31, 1776* (Edited with notes by Elizabeth Ellery Dana, Cambridge, 1924), *passim.*

6. *Adams Family Correspondence,* I, 119, 123.

7. See *Diary and Autobiography,* II, 96n and 97n. Adams's use of words is very interesting, not that of the twentieth century be it noted. See *Adams Family Correspondence,* I, 145. Charles Francis Adams, who said that the manuscript was defective at this point, wrote "recompense" instead of "reward" (*Familiar Letters,* p. 28).

8. Edmund Cody Burnett, *The Continental Congress* (Copyright 1941, New York, 1964), p. 19ff., Ch. 2, and p. 33 etc., is a summing-up of Burnett's life-time and classic work on the letters of members of the Congress. This work is hereafter referred to as Burnett, *Continental Congress.* See also footnote 10, below.

9. *Adams Family Correspondence,* I, 129, 164; *Diary and Autobiography,* II, 150, on the beer, the washing, and the morals and manners.

10. Burnett, *Continental Congress,* Ch. 4, *Diary and Autobiography,* II, 119. On the "Broadbrims," or Quakers, see *ibid.,* II, 107, 152, 155; *Adams Family Correspondence,* I, 157, 165; and for a later recollection, *Diary and Autobiography,* III, 311, 312. On the problem of religious dissension, see the last, II, 153n.

11. *Adams Family Correspondence,* I, 151n, 159, *Diary and Autobiography,* II, 124, Burnett, *Continental Congress,* pp. 39, 40.

12. Burnett, *Continental Congress*, p. 42ff., *Diary and Autobiography*, II, 135n.

13. The quotation is in *Adams Family Correspondence*, I, 159. See also Burnett, *Continental Congress*, p. 49, etc.

14. Merrill Jensen, *The Founding of a Nation, A History of the American Revolution 1763-1776* (New York, 1968), p. 499; Julian P. Boyd, *Anglo-American Union, Joseph Galloways's Plans to Preserve the British Empire, 1774-1788* (Copyright 1941, New York, Octagon Books, 1970), p. 32, hereafter referred to as Boyd, *Anglo-American Union*.

15. Boyd, *Anglo-American Union*, pp. 52, 53; (Intro. by Merrill Jensen), *Historical and Political Reflections on the Rise and Progress of the American Rebellion, by Joseph Galloway* (originally published in 1780, New York and London, 1972), xxii, hereafter referred to as Jensen, *Galloway's Reflections*. Page xxiv of this works refers to the felt need for a "balanced" government which Galloway, like John Adams and others in the eighteenth century, supported. The disagreement in 1774 about a "law of nature" being a basis for American rights (which Jensen says horrified "conservatives"), is also noted (p. xix). See *Diary and Autobiography*, II, 129, 141, 143, for Galloway's ideas at the time as reported by Adams; Galloway was obviously more political than philosophical. Perhaps he later became even more outspoken against a "law of nature" as suggested by his pamphleteering. Adams in his autobiographical recollection (*Diary and Autobiography*, III, 309) held that the "Law of Nature" was a "Resource" in 1774 to which the delegates might eventually be driven; but he had been plainly for it. Burnett, *Continental Congress*, p. 52, puts Adams in with the "philosophically minded members" of Congress at that time. The final report about rights does mention the laws of nature, but it makes them subordinate to the constitutional defense of Americans as Englishmen. (*Works*, II, 535ff. gives the original draught of rights and grievances and its final adoption in October.)

16. Burnett, *Continental Congress*, pp. 56, 57, quoting the Reverend Samuel Seabury of New York. This refers to Seabury's *Free Thoughts on the Proceedings of the Continental Congress* (1774), reprinted and edited with an introduction by Clarence H. Vance, *Letters of a Westchester Farmer 1774-1775, by Samuel Seabury* (The Westchester County Historical Society, White Plains, N.Y., 1930, New York, 1970). See also William H. Nelson, *The American Tory* (New York, 1961; Boston, 1964), p. 74ff., esp. p. 76.

17. *Adams Family Correspondence*, I, 183, 186n., also 251n. on the personnel of *The Group*.

18. On William Smith, see *ibid.*, 162n, and *ibid.*, II, 408 and note.

19. *Diary and Autobiography*, I, 161n., III, 313, 314, also *Works*, II, 405. The most recent study of the Massachusettensis-Novanglus controversy is by Bernard Mason, *The American Colonial Crisis, the Daniel Leonard-John Adams Letters to the Press, 1774-1795* (New York, 1972).

20. On the problem of the "realm," which the colonists frequently

mentioned (and which raised questions about the "empire"), see the classic work by Charles H. McIlwain, *The American Revolution, A Constitutional Interpretation* (Copyright 1923, New York, 1773). The Massachusetts General Court had made this argument as early as 1678. As to allegiance being due the king only in his "natural person," necessitating reciprocity in Adams's opinion, see "Novanglus" in *Works*, IV, 176, 177. On page 177 there is mention of another closely related constitutional point, that the settlers of Massachusetts had "brought their charter with them." See also p. 117 about the Massachusetts Council being unlike a House of Lords in legislative matters.

21. May 29, 1775, *Adams Family Correspondence*, I, 207.

22. *Ibid.*, 215; *Diary and Autobiography*, II, 162n.

23. *Ibid.*, 174n. on the intercepted letter which is quoted in *Works*, II, 411n. See also the latter work, p. 409ff., and the preceding footnote, on trouble with Dickinson.

24. See *Diary and Autobiography*, III, 326, 327.

25. For Adams's famous letter to James Sullivan, May 26, 1776, see *Works*, IX, 375ff. On Abigail and John Adams's attitude, see *Adams Family Correspondence*, I, 370, 382, 397, 402, II, 110. See also Whitney, *Abigail Adams*, pp. 129-131, and the preceding footnote.

26. On Paine, see *Adams Family Correspondence*, I, 348, 349n., and esp. p. 363 for John Adams's letter to Abigail on March 19.

27. The *Thoughts on Government* may be found in *Works*, IV, 193ff., and in *The Political Writings of John Adams, Representative Selections*, George A. Peek, Jr., ed., (New York, 1954) p. 83ff. Abigail's letter of November 27, 1775, about the need for laws, etc., is in *Adams Family Correspondence*, I, 329. Adams's remembrance of having insisted on a "balanced" government in Massachusetts in 1775 is confirmed in R. J. Taylor, ed., *Massachusetts, Colony to Commonwealth, Documents on the Formation of Its Constitution, 1775-1780* (Chapel Hill, 1961), p. 9.

28. See John A. Neuenschwander, *The Middle Colonies and the Coming of the Revolution* (Port Washington, N.Y., 1973), pp. 179, 195, 197, and esp. p. 214, hereafter referred to as Neuenschwander, *Middle Colonies*.

29. See *Diary and Autobiography*, III, 316.

30. Smith, *Adams*, I, 208, says that Elihu Adams died "suddenly and mysteriously." See also *Adams Family Correspondence*, I, 196, 196n.

31. See Adams's opinion in *Adams Family Correspondence*, I, 410, also "Thoughts" in *Works*, IV, 197.

32. Burnett, *Continental Congress*, esp. p. 150.

33. Adams to Rush in 1811, in *Spur of Fame*, p. 184.

34. On Dickinson and other moderates, see the quotation "like Grass before the Scythe" in John Adams's letter to Abigail, July 10, 1776, in *Adams Family Correspondence*, II, 42. On the irony of the Dickinson position, see Neuenschwander, *Middle Colonies*, p. 208, and, as it must have appeared to Galloway, Jensen, *Galloway's Reflections*, xxii. See also Jensen's *Articles of*

Confederation (Copyright 1940 by the Univ. of Wisconsin, Third edition, Madison, 1959), p. 126ff., "The Dickinson Draft of the Confederation."

35. See *Works*, I, 275, and *Adams Family Correspondence*, II, 372n., 375n., and *Works*, VII, 5-8.

Chapter Six

1. See the last footnote to the preceding chapter. On Deane, see R. A. East, *Business Enterprise in the American Revolutionary Era* (New York, 1938), pp. 127ff., 197, 198; and Adams's autobiographical recollection *(Diary and Autobiography*, III, 340) that Deane had always been a man of more ambition than of principle, etc. See also *Adams Family Correspondence*, IV, 231n. for a recent treatment of Deane.

2. See *Works*, I, 279; but see also Richard W. Van Alstyne, *Empire and Independence* (New York, London, Sydney, 1965), p. 163, hereafter referred to as Van Alstyne, *Empire and Independence*.

3. Felix Gilbert, *To the Farewell Address* (Copyright 1961, Princeton, 1970), *passim*, esp. 49ff., 87, hereafter referred to as Gilbert, *To the Farewell Address*. See also *Works*, X, 269, for Adams's old age remembrance of his ideas on neutrality in 1776. However, Adams did revert to his old ideas in making a treaty with Holland in 1782: Smith, *Adams*, I, 509.

4. See Van Alstyne, *Empire and Independence*, p. 163.

5. See *Adams Family Correspondence*, III, 170.

6. Richard B. Morris, *The Peacemakers, The Great Powers and America* (New York, 1965), pp. 112, 113, 191, hereafter referred to as Morris, *Peacemakers*. See also Chinard, *Adams*, p. 117. A more-or-less sympathetic account of Vergennes is given by Charles Francis Adams in *Works*, I, 299ff.

7. See *Diary and Autobiography*, IV, 69, 118, etc., also Abigail's letters in *Adams Family Correspondence*, IV, 164, 165, 179n., 230. Even in older age Adams showed his critical opinion of Franklin (*Works*, IX, 619) in saying that Franklin had once hated him, etc. See also Shaw, *Adams*, p. 279ff. for a summing up of Adams vs. Franklin very unfavorable to the former; and Smith, *Adams* II, 908, for Adams's later likening of Hamilton to Franklin in the field of moral behavior.

8. *Diary and Autobiography*, II, 361. Adams had read Molière when coming over in 1778: *Adams Family Correspondence*, I, 90n.

9. Smith, *Adams*, I, 429; *Diary and Autobiography*, IV, 125.

10. See *Diary and Autobiography*, II, 401n. "The Report of a Constitution" for Massachusetts, with John Adams's preliminary draft, is given in *Works*, IV, 219ff., preceded by "Observations" by Charles Francis Adams. See also *Adams Family Correspondence*, III, 228n.

11. *Works*, IV, 220; also Smith, *Adams*, I, 441. However, see also Chinard, *Adams*, p. 132, who speaks of the principles of the Declaration being reiterated with "modifications" suitable to the people of Massachusetts.

12. Smith, *Adams*, I, 440. See reference to this remarkable letter of Lee in *Adams Family Correspondence*, III, 235n.

13. See the long footnote in *Adams Family Correspondence*, III, 224ff., esp. 229. See also Smith, *Adams*, I, 445, for the "dirty work" of politics, which was an expression of James Lovell, referring to the treatment of Arthur Lee. See also, Chinard, *Adams*, p. 138.

14. Chinard, *Adams*, Book Two Ch. 2, "Shirt-sleeve Diplomacy," but see page 157.

15. See *Adams Family Correspondence*, III, 390n. to 395n., IV, 11. See also Smith, *Adams*, I, 472ff., Morris, *Peacemakers*, Ch. X, p. 191ff.

16. The famous Franklin quote is mentioned in *Diary and Autobiography*, I, lxiii. The correspondence to the *Patriot* in 1809–12 is discussed in detail in footnote 38 to Ch. 9. The official correspondence relating to this period is in *Works*, VII.

17. *Adams Family Correspondence*, III, 395n.

18. Chinard, *Adams*, p. 162.

19. See *Adams Family Correspondence*, III, xxxiv, IV, 244.

20. On Adams's relations with Livingston, see Chinard, *Adams*, p. 162; Smith, *Adams*, I, 506, and Gilbert, *To the Farewell Address*, pp. 82, 86.

21. *Adams Family Correspondence*, IV, 304n., 305n., 311.

22. *Ibid.*, p. 365.

23. On Shelburne succeeding Rockingham, see Morris, *Peacemakers*, p. 280; on Adams's thinking that his English newspaper writing had influenced Englishmen, see Van Alstyne, *Empire and Independence*, p. 214, and *Diary and Autobiography*, III, 80n. On the international situation influencing the British, see especially Piers Mackesy, *The War for America, 1775-1783* (Cambridge, 1965), pp. 474, 476, 505-08, etc. Jay and Adams are not even mentioned by name in the peace negotiations in this account, which is written from a Whitehall or Foreign Office point of view (and does not pretend to be a history of the "War for Independence," xvi); but it does mention Franklin on page 474, and refers to the American Commissioners as "schrewd, hard men" on page 506.

24. See Shaw, *Adams*, pp. 160, 161.

25. Morris, *Peacemakers*, p. 310; see also Smith, *Adams*, I, 539, 540 about the "Instructions."

26. Chinard, *Adams*, p. 176; Smith, *Adams*, I, 548.

27. On the Loyalists, see Van Alstyne, *Empire and Independence*, p. 220, and Morris, *Peacemakers*, p. 375. On Franklin's intransigence towards the Tories, see *Diary and Autobiography*, III, 77; but Morris, *Peacemakers*, p. 264, speaks of Franklin's earlier interest to compensate the Loyalists, as well as Patriotic sufferers, by getting Canada (*ibid.*, p. 262).

28. February 18, 1783. *Diary and Autobiography*, III, 108. See Chinard, *Adams*, p. 178.

29. See the charming *The Adams Family in Auteuil, 1784-1785, As Told in the Letters of Abigail Adams* (Boston, 1956), with an introduction and

notes by Howard C. Rice, Jr.

30. On Tyler and "Nabby" and the cooling off period being a "wise move," see *ibid.*, p. 3. See also my *John Quincy Adams, The Critical Years, 1785-1794* (New York, 1962), pp. 27, 28; *Earliest Diary*, 18ff., esp. 22n., 26ff., *Adams Family Correspondence*, 335ff.; *Diary and Autobiography*, III, 217n. On Colonel William Stephens Smith, see *ibid.*, III, 183n. and Katharine A. Roof, *Colonel William Smith and Lady, The Romance of Washington's Aide and Young Abigail Adams* (Boston, 1929), *passim*. On the history of the Borland, or Vassall, house, see esp. *Adams Family Correspondence*, III, 65n., 266n.

31. See Chinard, *Adams*, p. 194ff.; see also *Letters of Mrs. Adams, The Wife of John Adams*, Charles Francis Adams, ed. (Boston, 1848), p. 251ff. for an account of the English experience.

32. It apparently was so. See Smith, *Adams*, II, 638, 639, 677, etc.

33. See Sewall's letter of 1787 in *Works*, I, 57n., 58n.; also *Adams Family Correspondence*, I, 136n. and Smith, *Adams*, II, 645.

34. The *Defence* may be found in *Works*, IV, V, VI. What follows is based primarily on Chinard, *Adams*, p. 203ff. See also Smith, *Adams*, II, 690ff. The reference to Deane is in *Diary and Autobiography*, IV, 74n., and it was Abigail who called him a "Wretch."

35. See *Works*, p. 559.

36. See Chinard, *Adams*, p. 217.

34. See Smith, *Adams*, II, 734, 735. On page 923 of this work reference is made to Abigail's use of the Quincy coat of arms.

Chapter Seven

1. Smith, *Adams*, II, 735, 736.

2. *Works*, IX, 557.

3. Smith, *Adams*, II, 740.

4. *Ibid.*, pp. 726, 768, quoting from the Adams Papers microfilm; and *Works*, VIII, 464, 467, IX, 573. See also Adams's conclusion to the third volume of the *Defence*, *Works*, VI, 219, 220. Samuel Eliot Morison, ed., *Sources and Documents Illustrating the American Revolution, 1764-1788, and the Formation of the Federal Constitution* (Second Edition, Oxford, 1929), xliii, echoes Madison: "It was called the Federal rather than the National Constitution in order to disarm state prejudices against a 'consolidated' government." An observation recently made on the "national" character of the new constitution, is by Cecelia M. Kenyon, ed., *The Antifederalists* (Indianapolis, 1966), lvn. See also xxvi, on a possible change in people's thinking about republicanism after 1776 to one of "rigidity."

5. See my *John Quincy Adams*, p. 95, on his son's opinions. The quotation is from Smith, *Adams*, II, 755, in reply to a letter from Benjamin Rush in 1789 which charged Adams with leaning to monarchy; see Adams's statement to Rush, about the same time, denying an attachment to monarchy

and denying having changed his principles since 1776: *Works,* IX, 566.

6. See Manning J. Dauer, *The Adams Federalists* (originally published in 1953, Third Edition, Baltimore, 1968), p. 78ff. and esp. p. 82, hereafter referred to as Dauer, *Adams Federalists;* also John C. Miller, *The Federalist Era* (New York, 1963), p. 5ff., hereafter referred to as Miller, *Federalist Era.*

7. Smith, *Adams,* II, 742.

8. Smith, *Adams,* II, 758, 789.

9. Both the "Davila" and the letters to Sam Adams and to Roger Sherman are in *Works,* VI.

10. See Smith, *Adams,* II, 785, 786, 797, 831, etc. See also Chinard, *Adams,* p. 238ff., 249.

11. On the "Publicola" quarrel, Chinard, *Adams,* p. 238, applies the word "disingenuous" to Jefferson's letter of August 30, 1791. However, Charles Francis Adams implied something stronger in *Works,* VIII, 509n., 510n., and said so in *Works,* I, 618, 619. See also my *John Quincy Adams,* p. 146, and Smith, *Adams,* II, 819, who also uses the word "disingenuous" as applying to Jefferson on this occasion.

12. Dauer, *Adams Federalists,* p. 87, gives the electoral figures for 1792. See also Miller, *Federalist Era,* pp. 122ff. Edward Channing, *A History of the United States* (six vols., 1905-1925), IV, 171, characterizes Adams as a man of "honest, and open ways." This work is hereafter referred to as Channing, *History.*

13. Smith, *Adams,* II, 813. This criticism of Jefferson was because he had been seen at the lodgings of a Clinton supporter.

14. *Ibid.,* p. 845.

15. *Works,* IX, 638, is from a letter written in 1811 but it accurately sums up his earlier attitude. See also Smith, *Adams,* II, 1085.

16. Smith, *Adams,* II, 758.

17. Channing, *History,* IV, 142ff.; Miller, *Federalist Era,* pp. 140, 164ff.

18. Smith, *Adams,* II, 875. An interesting argument, that the "pro-French" Republicans were really, in the last analysis, nationalistic and isolationist, is made by Lawrence S. Kaplan, "Toward Isolationism: the Jeffersonian Republicans and the Franco-American Alliance of 1778," in *Historical Reflections,* IV, January, 1977, p. 69ff.

19. East, *John Quincy Adams,* p. 180.

20. See Miller, *Federalist Era,* p. 129.

21. Stephen G. Kurtz, *The Presidency of John Adams, The Collapse of Federalism 1795-1800* (Copyright 1957, New York, 1961), p. 80, hereafter referred to as Kurtz, *Presidency of John Adams.*

22. Smith, *Adams,* II, 905, on Adams's "need."

23. Channing, *History,* IV, 173.

24. *Ibid.,* p. 217; Chinard, *Adams,* p. 257. See also Kurtz, *Presidency of John Adams,* pp. 201ff.

25. Chinard, *Adams,* 257; Smith, *Adams,* II, 906.

26. Smith, *Adams,* II, 894.

Chapter Eight

1. Kurtz, *Presidency of John Adams, passim,* esp. Ch. 5, and appendices. On Adams having been President "by accident," see Channing, *History,* IV, 217, but also Kurtz, p. 201.

2. For Adams's recollection (1815) about Burr, see *Works,* X, 124. See also Miller, *Federalist Era,* pp. 201, 202; Kurtz, *Presidency of John Adams,* pp. 94, 197, 328; Dauer, *Adams Federalists,* pp. 218, 219.

3. Kurtz, *Presidency of John Adams,* p. 200.

4. Channing, *History,* IV, 46.

5. Kurtz, *Presidency of John Adams,* p. 283; Smith, *Adams,* II, 1030.

6. Kurtz, *Presidency of John Adams,* p. 49, Pro- and anti-French divisions seem to have influenced American opinion from 1778 on.

7. See Chinard, *Adams,* p. 261, and Miller, *Federalist Era,* p. 244. Kurtz, *Presidency of John Adams,* pp. 279, 281, 283, thinks that Adams did not personally dislike any of Washington's secretaries, and that he was "patient" and "lenient" with them for a long time.

8. Smith, *Adams,* II, 920, 928. He says on page 930 that Republicans at first thought that Adams was simply Thomas Jefferson in disguise.

9. Adams's remark about "stupid" is in Smith, *Adams,* II, 933. See also Channing, *History,* IV, 314, 360.

10. Smith, *Adams,* II, 923; Kurtz, *Presidency of John Adams,* pp. 228, 229.

11. On Talleyrand, see Smith, *Adams,* II, 953, Miller, *Federalist Era,* 243.

12. Kurtz, *Presidency of John Adams,* p. 324.

13. Miller, *Federalist Era,* p. 229, says that neither Adams nor Hamilton inspired the so-called "Alien and Sedition Acts."

14. *New Letters of Abigail Adams,* Stewart Mitchell, ed. (Boston, 1947), pp. 159, 165, 172, 179, 193, 196.

15. Chinard, *Adams,* p. 289ff., 298ff. Adams was, of course, charged with being "pro-French," but he himself (p. 304) accused one of his cabinet members as having been "pro-British." There had been some justification for Pickering's attitude in 1799 to suspend all negotiations until there were further developments (p. 289).

16. Smith, *Adams,* II, 923, on Abigail's use of the Quincy coat-of-arms on her carriage.

17. On Charles, *ibid.,* pp. 875, 876, 988, 1015, 1037, 1049; on Nabby and her husband, *ibid.,* pp. 991, 992. The quote from Aunt Eliza is from my *John Quincy Adams,* p. 125.

18. On William Smith, the brother of Abigail, see *Adams Family Correspondence,* IV, 98 and especially Chapter 5, footnote 18, of this work; also my *John Quincy Adams,* p. 238. (The "little tribe of girls" referred to there should have included at least one son.)

19. See my *John Quincy Adams,* p. 122ffl., esp. 127, Ch. 7, and p. 170.

20. Kurtz, *Presidency of John Adams,* pp. 393, 395, 397. Chinard. *Adams,*

p. 300 speaks of Adams's trip to Virginia and of some people's political interpretation thereof, but on page 307 he speaks of Adams as being no "party chief."

21. Miller, *Federalist Era,* p. 202, speaks of the sectional feeling in 1796, and on page 268 says of the election of 1800 that "party discipline" made a remarkable display. See also, on page 267, Miller's indictment of Charles Pinckney in 1800, who, by "dint of liberal promises of patronage (which Jefferson later duly honored), to the members of the South Carolina legislature. . . ." The quote of Adams about Federalists is in Smith, *Adams,* II, 1053. See also Kurtz, *Presidency of John Adams,* p. 394. Adams himself, on one occasion, blamed South Carolina for having turned him out in 1800 by votes "not fairly obtained." (*Spur of Fame,* p. 225).

22. Channing, *History,* IV, 219; Kurtz, *Presidency of John Adams,* p. 406; Miller, *Federalist Era,* p. 274.

23. See footnote 21, above. On Adams's recollection (1815) about the Muhlenbergs in Pennsylvania in 1800, see *Works,* X, 122, but this sort of thing defies analysis. Adams also said in 1807 that the Virginians had persuaded Burr to "corrupt" the State of New York; *Spur of Fame,* p. 78.

24. Channing, *History,* IV, 173. On Adams's behavior in leaving before the inauguration in 1801, see Chinard, *Adams,* p. 314, and Smith, *Adams,* II, 1066. The interpretation above is my own, following Channing. On page 300, when referring to an earlier event, Chinard criticizes Adams as "too much a schoolmaster."

Chapter Nine

1. Chinard, *Adams,* p. 317, who says that Adams's tongue had "lost none of its sharpness." Anyone who doubts it is invited to read this chapter.

2. For a history of the *Autobiography,* see *Diary and Autobiography,* I, xliv, lxviii.

3. See footnote 21, below.

4. See *Works,* X, 148, 151, and footnote 38, below.

5. The quotation about history is from a letter to Rush in 1809, *Spur of Fame,* p. 152. For a full citation of this work see Chapter 1, footnote 22.

6. *Works,* IX, 582.

7. Smith, *Adams,* II, 1071.

8. *Spur of Fame, passim.*

9. Quoted in Chinard, *Adams,* p. 321.

10. *Ibid.,* p. 318.

11. Smith, *Adams,* II, 1094.

12. *Works,* IX, 631; Smith, *Adams,* II, 1096.

13. Smith, *Adams,* II, 1094, 1110; *Spur of Fame,* p. 135n.

14. Smith, *Adams,* II, 1094.

15. *Ibid.,* p. 1068.

16. *Spur of Fame,* p. 34 and note.

17. *Ibid.,* p. 48.

18. Chinard, *Adams,* p. 162.

19. See my *Business Enterprise in the American Revolutionary Era* (1938, New York), *passim.*

20. Published in Boston in 1805.

21. *Correspondence Between John Adams and Mercy Warren* (C. F. Adams [Jr.], ed.), *with an appendix of Specimen Pages from the History* (Reprinted by the Arno Press, New York, 1972, from a copy in the State Historical Society of Wisconsin, first printed in the *Collections of the Massachusetts Historical Society,* Vol. IV, 5th Series, 1878). This work is hereafter referred to as *Correspondence with Mercy Warren.*

22. *Correspondence with Mercy Warren,* p. 451, also page 359.

23. *Ibid.,* p. 480.

24. *Ibid.,* p. 498, for Gerry's observation. See also Chapter 3 of this work.

25. *Correspondence with Mercy Warren,* p. 338ff.

26. *Ibid.,* p. 352.

27. *Ibid.,* pp. 360, 363.

28. *Ibid.,* pp. 329, 360.

29. *Ibid.,* p. 354.

30. *Ibid.,* pp. 479, 490.

31. *Spur of Fame,* p. 24. The observation had been made by two of his intimate friends, Sewall and Leonard (both of whom turned out to be Loyalists).

32. *Ibid.,* pp. 104, 113, 135, 184, 229, also p. 283 for editors' comment.

33. *Ibid.,* p. 217; see also p. 35.

34. *Ibid.,* pp. 243, 244.

35. *Ibid.,* p. 170.

36. *Ibid.,* p. 281.

37. *Ibid.,* p. 202.

38. *Correspondence of the Late President Adams, Originally published in the Boston Patriot* (published by Everett and Munroe, No. 78 State Street, Boston, 1809) consists of communications sent in by John Adams in 1809, but his reminiscences in the *Patriot* continued until 1812. See *Diary and Correspondence,* I, liv, lxxii, II, 458n., III, 41n.; also *Adams Family Correspondence,* III, 411n. John Adams wrote in 1815 (*Works,* X, 148) that a grandson of his had had his communications to the *Patriot* relating to the missions to France bound up in a pamphlet. See also Shaw, *Adams,* pp. 149n., 295ff. Some of the communications in 1811 were used by Charles Francis Adams as appendices to support observations made about his grandfather in the "Life" in *Works,* I (notably on the peace negotiations of 1782 and the inclusion of Maine's extreme limits). He also reproduced some of John Adams's remarks in the *Patriot* in 1809 in *Works,* IX, beginning on page 241 but with a preliminary note on pages 239 and 240.

John Adams seems to have had two objects in sending this material to the *Patriot* between 1809 and 1812: to refute Hamilton's charges in 1800, and to rebuke Franklin for his attitude in 1781 and 1782.

39. Adams's letters to John Taylor of Caroline, Va., in 1814, can be found in *Works*, VI, 447, with an "Editor's Preface."

40. One treatment is that by D. H. Stewart and G. P. Clarke, "Misanthrope or Humanitarian? John Adams in Retirement," *New England Quarterly*, XXVIII (1955).

41. See the *Familiar Letters*, xxix, for a letter written by Abigail in 1814. See also Smith, *Adams*, II, 1099, 2000, for later details.

42. Smith, *Adams*, II, 1073, 1074.

Chapter Ten

1. On the "quiveration," or palsy, see Chinard, *Adams*, p. 344, and on Sam Adams, the same; on the "quiveration" see also *Spur of Fame*, p. 186. On Adams's loss of teeth as early as 1798, see Smith, *Adams*, II, 990.

2. Andrew Oliver, *Portraits of John and Abigail Adams* (Cambridge, 1967), p. 189 (page 203 on the "cigar"), hereafter referred to as Oliver, *Portraits*.

3. Smith, *Adams*, II, 1070, 1119, 1124, etc., but he also told them to study hard and to cultivate virtue (*ibid.*, p. 1117).

4. Smith, *Adams*, II, 1100, 1113, 1114.

5. *Ibid.*, p. 1122. See also Chinard, *Adams*, p. 339, and his *Thomas Jefferson, Apostle of Americanism* (Copyright 1929, Ann Arbor, 1957), p. 519.

6. Oliver, *Portraits*, p. 189 on Stuart (the portrait is on page 190), p. 147 on Morse (the "stern" portrait is on p. 148) and p. 202ff. on Browere (the life mask is on pp. 204, 205).

7. Chinard, *Adams*, pp. 332-37.

8. *Ibid.*, pp. 334-37. Smith, *Adams*, II, 1078.

9. Chinard, *Adams*, pp. 334, 336ff., esp. 339, 340.

10. On the art of lawgiving, see *Works*, X, 398. On Adams's experience of music, see *Diary and Autobiography*, I, 281, II, 31, IV, 119, etc.; also Smith, *Adams*, II, 716.

11. *Works*, X, 41.

12. *Ibid.*, p. 247. See also footnote 17, below.

13. *Ibid.*, pp. 394, 395.

14. *Ibid.*, p. 379.

15. *Ibid.*, p. 359ff.

16. *Ibid.*, p. 377.

17. *Ibid.*, pp. 350, 351, 355.

18. See his important letter to William Tutor, March 7, 1819, in *Works*, X, p. 367ff., esp. p. 375.

19. *Ibid.*, pp. 367-69.

20. *Spur of Fame*, p. 80ff. gives Adams's letter to Nathan Webb in 1755 (see also *Works*, IX, 591) on which his claim in old age was based; but see also

editors' comment in this work, p. 83n.

21. *Diary and Autobiography,* I, 65, furnishes an early, interesting observation on Peter. See Smith, *Adams,* II, 1130 for the episode recorded above. Smith, *ibid.,* p. 1098, gives Adams's reflections on Americans as a peace loving people.

22. Smith, *Adams,* II, 1131.

23. For Charles Francis Adams's remarks, see *Works,* I, 633. See also *Spur of Fame,* p. 173, for his reading in 1810.

24. *Works,* X, 403.

25. Chinard, *Adams,* pp. 340, 341; Smith, *Adams,* II, 1129.

26. *Works,* I, 639ff. for Charles Francis Adams's summary.

Selected Bibliography

The problem of writing about John Adams is complicated by the release in microfilm of the Adams Papers at the Massachusetts Historical Society. Fortunately, much of this is given in Page Smith's biography of John Adams, mentioned below, and in the expert editing by Lyman H. Butterfield and others in modern editions of the writing and scribbling by John and Abigail and by members and friends of the family, also mentioned below. Some of this material I remember in the preparation of my own account of the early years of John Quincy Adams, as stated in the Preface.

It should be noted that there is almost nothing in John Adams's diary or in his autobiographical recollection about his Presidency or his retirement in Quincy. There is also a special danger because of the gaps in the diary. To what extent any diary is revealing is, of course, anybody's guess; and, as Charles Francis Adams said, "No true, honestly written Diary can be regarded as in itself a correct generally written history." I have attempted to show the importance of one of those gaps—always acknowledged by editors but still a problem—in my "The Strange Pause in John Adams's Diary," in *Toward a New View of America: Essays in Honor of Arthur C. Cole,* edited by Hans L. Trefousse (New York, 1977).

The beginning of all wisdom about John Adams and most primary material about him is found in the ten volume edition of his works published by his grandson, Charles Francis Adams, in the middle of the nineteenth century: *The Works of John Adams, Second President of the United States, with a Life of the Author* . . . (10 vols., Boston, 1850-1856). Most of the *Life* in the first volume was written by the editor himself, but the account of the early years of John Adams was written by his eldest son, John Quincy Adams, our Sixth President; and in several appendices to this first volume, and in Volume Nine, there is a part of the material sent by John Adams in 1809-1812 to the Boston *Patriot,* sometimes called his "second auto-biography." The *Life* itself was republished in 1874: *The Life of John Adams. Begun by John Quincy Adams. Completed by Charles Francis Adams. Revised and Corrected* (2 vols., Philadelphia, 1874). Biographies of John Adams have otherwise been curiously few until very recently.

What follows is an attempt to make intelligible the almost endless information about John Adams by a discussion of original material about him, in addition to listing books and articles mentioned in the footnotes. Modern interest in publishing "letterpress" material, while admirable in itself, in some ways complicates an understanding of history. To publish "original" material often makes a scholar wonder just what has been omitted, or what has been unavailable because it has disappeared. We sometimes seem like the White Queen in *Through the Looking Glass:* we have to run twice as fast in order to stay in the same place. Even when, as in the case of the Adams Papers, microfilming is a first step, there remains a problem. "Selecting" the items to appear in print, and how they should be arranged, thus influencing "public opinion," will always be serious questions for scholars.

PUBLISHED ADAMS MATERIAL

Of course the most famous of all editing about John Adams was that by Charles Francis Adams in preparing the ten volume edition of the *Works,* published in Boston between 1850 and 1856 (also available in reprint), as noted above. It has been the backbone of this work.

Since there are various editions of a *Dissertation on the Canon and Feudal Law* (1765) and of the *Thoughts on Government* (1776), a survey might best begin with John Adams's *Defence of the Constitutions of Government of the United States of America,* 3 vols., published in London, the first in 1787. (The spelling of the *Defence* should be noted carefully for it is not the way we spell "defense" today, and is of course a "defense" of state constitutions and *not,* as is sometimes unfortunately stated, a "defense" of the Constitution of the Federal government.) Numerous newspaper articles of John Adams could also be put here, but the *Correspondence of the Late President Adams. Originally Published in the Boston Patriot. In a Series of Letters,* Boston, Everett and Munroe, 1809, is a real book, whereas Adams's writings "On Davila," for example, printed a few years before, are nothing but old newspaper articles of 1790.

Adams's correspondence with William Cunningham (printed in Boston for political reasons in 1823), and with Professor John Winthrop in the *Collections of the Massachusetts Historical Society,* 5th ser., vol. 4, Boston, 1878, and with Benjamin Waterhouse, edited by Worthington C. Ford, Boston, 1927 (in a book called *Statesman and Friend*), should also be noted. Especially revealing is the work recently edited by John Schutz and Douglass Adair, *The Spur of Fame: Dialogues of John Adams and Benjamin Rush, 1805-1813,* the Huntington Library, San Marino, California, 1966.

The Correspondence Between John Adams and Mercy Warren, edited by Charles Francis Adams (Jr.) was originally printed in the *Collections of the Massachusetts Historical Society* for 1878, but has been republished in its revised form in New York in 1972, with an appendix of specimen pages from Mrs. Warren's *History,* as a part of the series *American Women, Images and Realities.* There might be added here, Charles Warren, ed., *Warren-Adams Letters: Being Chiefly a Correspondence among John Adams, Samuel Adams, and James Warren,* 2 vols., Boston, 1917-1925.

The Letters of John Adams, Addressed to His Wife, edited by his grandson, Charles Francis Adams, 2 vols., Boston, 1841, was subsequently used for the *Familiar Letters of John Adams and His Wife Abigail Adams During the Revolution*, which was prepared for the Centennial celebration and published in New York and Boston in 1876.

Charles Francis Adams also selected and edited the *Letters of Mrs. Adams, the Wife of John Adams*, with a Memoir of Abigail, in 1841. The famous fourth edition of this work (1848) contained "John Quincy Adams's Letters to His Son on the Study of the Bible." It was also used by Charles Francis Adams in the *Familiar Letters* some thirty years later. *New Letters of Abigail Adams*, Boston, 1947, was edited by Stewart Mitchell.

Writings by children of John and Abigail Adams have also sometimes been put into print, notably the *Journal and Correspondence of Miss Adams, Daughter of John Adams . . . edited by Her Daughter*, 2 vols., New York and London, 1841-42. *The Writings of John Quincy Adams* (the eldest son and our Sixth President) were edited by W. C. Ford in seven volumes in New York after 1913, but were cut off in 1917. The *Memoirs* of John Quincy Adams, in twelve volumes, had been edited by Charles Francis Adams and published in Philadelphia beginning in 1874. John Quincy Adams's diary for 1787, when he was a student in the law office of Theophilus Parsons of Newburyport, was edited for publication by Charles Francis Adams (Jr.), with the assistance of Miss J. C. Watts, in Boston in 1903.

Editions of the Adams-Jefferson correspondence have appeared in modern times, under the editorship of Paul Wilstach and Lester Capon, respectively.

The most recent development has been the editing that has come from the Adams Papers in the Massachusetts Historical Society, where they had been deposited by the Adams family some fifty years before. These include the *Diary and Autobiography of John Adams*, Lyman H. Butterfield, ed., L. C. Faber and W. D. Garrett, asst. eds., 4 vols., Cambridge, 1961; *The Earliest Diary of John Adams*, L. H. Butterfield, ed., W. D. Garrett and M. Friedlaender, assoc. eds., (containing material subsequently found in the Royall Tyler Collection in the Vermont Historical Society in Montpelier, presumably taken by Tyler when he had had access to John Adams's library in the 1780's when he was engaged to Nabby Adams); and *The Adams Family Correspondence*, 4 vols., Cambridge, 1965-1973, L. H. Butterfield, ed., W. D. Garrett, assoc. ed., M. E. Sprague, asst. ed. for the first two volumes, and L. H. Butterfield and Marc Friedlaender, eds. for the third and fourth volumes.

Andrew Oliver has also published *Portraits of John and Abigail Adams*, Cambridge, 1967, in this series; as have K. Worth and H. Zobel, eds., *The Legal Papers of John Adams*, 3 vols., Cambridge, 1968. Recently, but not used in the text, has begun to appear *The Papers of John Adams*, Vols. I and II to April, 1775, 2 vols. to date, Cambridge, 1977, under the editorship of Robert J. Taylor, Mary-Jo Kline, assoc. ed., and Gregg L. Lint, asst. ed.

Several other letters of John Adams are scattered in the publications of various learned societies.

BOOKS AND ARTICLES MENTIONED IN THE FOOTNOTES

ADAMS, CHARLES FRANCIS Jr. *Three Episodes of Massachusetts History,* 2 vols., revised, copyright 1892, New York, 1965.

ADAMS, RANDOLPH G. *Political Ideas of the American Revolution,* with Commentary by Merrill Jensen. Third Edition, New York, 1958, first published in 1922 by Trinity College, Durham, esp. ch. 5, "John Adams as a Britannic Statesman."

BERKIN, CAROL. *Jonathan Sewall, Odyssey of an American Loyalist,* New York, 1974.

BOWEN, CATHERINE DRINKER. *John Adams and the American Revolution,* Boston, 1949.

BOYD, JULIAN P. *Anglo-American Union: Joseph Galloway's Plans to Preserve the British Empire, 1744-1788.* Philadelphia, 1941; rpt. New York: Octagon Books, 1970.

BROWN, RICHARD D. *Revolutionary Politics in Massachusetts: The Boston Committee of Correspondence and the Towns, 1772-1774,* Cambridge, 1970.

BURNETT, EDMUND CODY. *The Continental Congress,* New York, 1941.

CHANNING, EDWARD. *A History of the United States,* 6 vols. New York, 1905-1925.

CHINARD, GILBERT. *Honest John Adams,* Boston, 1933.

COLBOURN, H. TREVOR. *The Lamp of Experience, Whig History and the Intellectual Origins of the American Revolution,* 1965; rpt. New York, 1974.

DANA, ELIZABETH ELLERY. *The British in Boston, Being the Diary of Lieutenant John Barker of the King's Own Regiment from November 15, 1774 to May 31, 1776,* edited with notes by Elizabeth Ellery Dana, Cambridge, 1924.

DAUER, MANNING J. *The Adams Federalists,* Baltimore, 1953.

EAST, ROBERT A. *John Quincy Adams, The Critical Years, 1785-1794,* New York, 1962.
     "The Strange Pause in John Adams's Diary," in *Toward a New View of America: Essays in Honor of Arthur C. Cole,* Hans Trefousse, ed., New York, 1977.

GILBERT, FELIX. *To the Farewell Address, Ideas of Early American Foreign Policy,* Princeton, 1961.

HARASZTI, ZOLTAN. *John Adams and the Prophets of Progress,* Cambridge, 1962.

HOWE, JOHN R. Jr. *The Changing Political Thought of John Adams,* Princeton, 1966.

JENSEN, MERRILL. *The Articles of Confederation, An Interpretation of the Social-Constitutional History of the American Revolution, 1774-1781,* copyright by the University of Wisconsin, 1940; third printing, Madison, 1959.

Historical and Political Reflections on the Rise and Progress of the American Rebellion, by Joseph Galloway, 1780, rpt. with a new introduction by Merrill Jensen, New York and London, 1972.

The Founding of a Nation, A History of the American Revolution 1763-1776, New York, 1968.

KAPLAN, LAWRENCE S. "Toward Isolation: the Jeffersonian Republicans and the Franco-American Alliance of 1778," in *Historical Reflections,* IV, January, 1977.

KENYON, CECELIA M. ed. *The Antifederalists,* Indianapolis, 1966.

KURTZ, STEPHEN G. *The Presidency of John Adams: The Collapse of Federalism 1795-1800,* Philadelphia, 1957.

LEVENTHAL, HERBERT. *In the Shadow of the Enlightenment: Occultism and Renaissance Science in Eighteenth-Century America,* New York, 1976.

MACKESY, PIERS. *The War For America, 1775-1783,* Cambridge, 1965.

MCILWAIN, CHARLES HOWARD. *The American Revolution, A Constitutional Interpretation,* copyright 1923, rpt. New York, 1973.

MASON, BERNARD. *The American Colonial Crisis, the Daniel Leonard-John Adams Letters to the Press, 1774-1775,* New York, 1972.

MILLER, JOHN C. *The Federalist Era, 1789-1801,* copyright 1960; rpt. New York, 1963.

MORGAN, EDMUND S. and HELEN M. *The Stamp Act Crisis, Prologue to Revolution,* copyright 1953; rpt. New York, 1963.

MORISON, SAMUEL ELIOT, ed. *Sources and Documents Illustrating the American Revolution, 1764-1788, and the Formation of the Federal Constitution,* Oxford, 1929.

MORRIS, RICHARD B. *The Peacemakers: The Great Powers and American Independence,* New York, 1965.

NEUENSCHWANDER, JOHN A. *The Middle Colonies and the Coming of the American Revolution,* Port Washington, 1973.

OLIVER, ANDREW. *Portraits of John and Abigail Adams,* Cambridge, 1967.

PATTERSON, STEPHEN E. *Political Parties in Revolutionary Massachusetts,* Madison, 1973.

SHAW, PETER. *The Character of John Adams,* Chapel Hill, 1976.

SMITH, PAGE. *John Adams,* 2 vols. New York, 1962.

STEWART, D. H. and G. P. CLARKE. "Misanthrope or Humanitarian? John Adams in Retirement," *New England Quarterly,* XXVIII (1955).

VAN ALSTYNE, RICHARD W. *Empire and Independence: The International History of the American Revolution,* New York, 1965.

WATERS, JOHN J. *The Otis Family in Provincial and Revolutionary Massachusetts,* Chapel Hill, 1968.

WHITNEY, JANET. *Abigail Adams,* Boston, 1947.

ZOBEL, HILLER B. "Newer Light on the Boston Massacre," *Proceedings of the American Antiquarian Society,* April, 1968.

Index